T0098182

Pioneers of Religious Zionism

Rabbis Alkalai, Kalischer, Mohliver, Reines, Kook and Maimon

PIONEERS OF RELIGIOUS ZIONISM

RABBIS ALKALAI, KALISCHER, MOHLIVER, REINES, KOOK AND MAIMON

RAYMOND GOLDWATER

URIM PUBLICATIONS
Jerusalem • New York

Pioneers of Religious Zionism: Rabbis Alkalai, Kalischer, Mohliver, Reines, Kook and Maimon
By Raymond Goldwater
Photos of Rabbis courtesy of Mossad HaRav Kook, Jerusalem

Copyright © 2009 by Raymond Goldwater
All rights reserved. No part of this book may be used or reproduced in any manner whatsoever without written permission from the copyright owner, except in the case of brief quotations embodied in reviews and articles.

Printed in Israel. First Edition.
ISBN 978-965-524-023-8
Urim Publications
P.O. Box 52287, Jerusalem 91521 Israel

Lambda Publishers Inc.
527 Empire Blvd., Brooklyn, New York 11225 U.S.A.
Tel: 718-972-5449 Fax: 718-972-6307, mh@ejudaica.com

www.UrimPublications.com

To my dear wife, Bella

CONTENTS

PREFACE

THIS BOOK DEALS with the life and thought of the six most important Zionist rabbis of the nineteenth and early twentieth centuries: Yehudah ben Shlomo Alkalai (1798–1878), Zvi Hirsch Kalischer (1795–1874), Samuel Mohliver (1824–1891), Jacob Reines (1839–1915), Abraham Isaac Kook (1865–1935) and Judah Leib (Fishman) Maimon (1875–1962). These rabbis combined traditional Jewish life and thought with practical Zionism.

Alkalai, a contemporary of Kalischer and a leader of the self-governing Jewish community in the Land of Israel, was the "prophet" of modern religious Zionism. He developed the concept of *teshuva* as meaning both repentance and return to the Land of Israel, the combination of which would lead to the full redemption. Alkalai also wrote practical proposals for the return of the Jewish People to its land that foreshadowed future developments in Zionism.

As we shall see, rabbinic reaction to Alkalai's ideas was mixed. Samson Raphael Hirsch rejected the basis of his ideas about resettlement of the Land of Israel and the full redemption which, in Hirsch's view, could occur only by divine intervention. In addition, Rabbi Meier Auerbach, the head of the Ashkenazi Beth Din in Jerusalem, disagreed with Alkaki's entire philosophy. Yet Alkalai was not only a theorist; he was also was a man of practical affairs. He sent his son to investigate conditions in the land of Israel and traversed Europe in order to raise funds to support the nascent settlements there.

Mohliver foreshadowed later developments within the Zionist movement by working with the secular Chovevei Zion group, for which he raised money and became spokesman to Jewish philanthropists. In order to relieve the strain in Chovevei Zion, Mohliver founded a spiritual center within the organization in order to spread the idea of settlement in Eretz Israel among the religious population. This center later became the Mizrachi Movement.

It is therefore a paradox that Jacob Reines, who founded Mizrachi as a religious party within the Zionist movement, rejected the concept central to the thought of Alkalai and Kalischer: that the purpose of settling Eretz Israel was to establish a self-governing community there in order to bring about the final redemption. Reines disagreed, believing that the redemption could only come about by divine intervention. For him, modern religious Zionism was a solution to the two great problems that world Jewry faced: assimilation and persecution. Consistent with this view, Reines was prepared to accept an offer by the British government of a Jewish national home in Uganda.

Rabbi Abraham Isaac Kook's assessment of Zionism was quite different. For him, the acquisition and settlement of land in Israel was a halachic imperative. He felt that dissatisfaction with the secular nature of most settlements did not exempt the Jewish people from their halachic duty to develop the land.

Judah Leib Maimon became active in the Mizrachi organization. Under his leadership the Mizrachi Movement became the constant ferment that infused modern Zionism with the concept of the divine. He believed that the synthesis of holy and secular thus created would produce the vitality necessary to ensure the success of Zionism (*Chazon ha-geulah,* 184–186). Through Maimon's complete identification with the aims of Zionism and attachment to the whole of the Jewish people, he was able to persuade the Zionist leaders and, later on, the political leaders of the newly-created State of Israel to meet the basic requirements of traditional Judaism in its public life.

The lives and thought of Rabbis Alkalai, Kalischer, Mohliver, Kook and Maimon provided the philosophical, religious and practical basis for Zionism, and ensured that the Zionist movement and the Jewish state would not become disconnected from Jewish tradition.

Rabbi Yehudah Ben Shlomo Chai Alkalai   הרב יהודה בן שלמה חי אלקלעי

Rabbi Yehudah Ben Shlomo Chai Alkalai (1798–1878)

Yehudah ben Shlomo Chai Alkalai was born in Sarajevo, Bosnia in 1798. He spent his youth in Jerusalem, where he was influenced by Rabbi Eliezer Papo, himself a native of Sarajevo. He returned to Serbia as a young man where he eventually succeeded his father as cantor and teacher in Zemlin (Zemun), and he became the rabbi of the community at the age of twenty-seven. There he came under the influence of Rabbi Judah Samuel Bais, a founder of the Hibbat Zion movement, as his writings and articles in later years show clearly.

In order to understand Alkalai's life and work properly, we must look at the events in Europe and particularly in Serbia, which formed both the backdrop and the stimulus for his philosophy and action. The French Revolution had stimulated both individuals and peoples to demand freedom to develop indigenous cultures and shake off the political shackles imposed by the Turkish and Austro-Hungarian empires. But this flowering of national and individual freedom benefited Jews intermittently at best. Although Jews supported the independence movements, they were still subjected to periodic expulsions from cities or villages, restricted in professions or business and, despite an 1860 decree emancipating all citizens, were not given full emancipation.

As a teacher, Alkalai soon realized the necessity of a dictionary and grammar textbook for the teaching of Hebrew, and his first book, *Darchei Noam,* which was published in Ladino in 1839, met this need. In this work, Alkalai gave many examples of the serious textual distortions that result from the imprecise reading of individual Hebrew letters. The vast majority of rabbis at the time regarded knowledge of grammar as unimportant despite the example of Rabbi Eliyahu ben Shlomo Zalman, the Vilna Gaon (1720–1797), whose revolutionary understanding of the Talmud and elucidation of the text stemmed in part from his deep knowledge of Hebrew grammar.

Darchei Noam also gives an indication of Alkalai's views about the redemption of the Jewish People through the biblical and Talmudic texts and interpretations quoted to support his views. He stipulates three developments that are necessary before redemption can take place. First, people must increase their observance of the commandments, which he interpreted as giving one's heart to return to Eretz Israel, the place of Torah. For support, he quotes Leviticus 25:38: "… to give you the land of Canaan in order to be your God."

Secondly, he believed people must increase their donations to charity in fulfillment of the verse: "[T]o try with all our strength… to show that even the hearts of those of us who are outside the Land lovingly cleave to it and to those who dwell there." Third, he quotes the teaching of Isaac Abarbanel (1437–1508) that God ordered the construction of the Temple so that there would be a place for prayer. Thus, everyone who lives inside or outside the land must pray for the ingathering of the exiles speedily in our days, for the sake of God's Great Name.[1] Alkalai attributes great significance to the concepts of Torah, charity and prayer, with the return to Zion as the necessary first step of the Jewish people's redemption.

Alkalai's ideas came under fierce criticism in many rabbinical circles. In contrast to the Zionist rabbis of this time who simply decided that return to Zion was the only answer to the ongoing problems of assimilation and persecution, non-Zionist rabbis, particularly in Jerusalem, greeted his work with deafening silence. In this context, the appreciative letter that Sir Moses Montefiore wrote to him must have been some consolation (*op. cit.*, 18).

In the following year, 1840, he published his second work, *Shelom Yerushalayim*, which set out some of his basic ideas for the first time. His approach to the redemption of the Jewish people lay in his concept of the Josephian (or preparatory) Messiah and the Davidian (the ultimate) Messiah. Alkalai writes that the first is a precursor of the second and will

---

[1] *Kitvei ha-Rav Alkalai,*Mosad Ha'Rav Kook, 21–22.

arrive through the efforts of the Jewish people, and this theme acts as a *leitmotif* in his later writings. He also called on the Jewish people to do *teshuvah* and stressed the necessity of tithing (setting aside ten percent of one's assets and income for charity) to support settlement efforts in the Land of Israel, saying, "Redemption will only come through tithe" (*op. cit.*, 195). He wrote that poverty in Eretz Israel should be no impediment to aliyah: "Wealth and blessing will increase in our land and livelihood will be abundantly available" (*op. cit.*, 183).

The Damascus Affair of 1840 in which thirteen Jews were falsely accused of murdering a Christian monk in order to use his blood to bake matzah for Passover affected Alkalai deeply and sent shock waves through the Jewish world. It is probably no accident that in the same year, Alkalai set out his basic ideas for the redemption of the Jewish People in his work *Minchat Yehudah*.

The second paragraph of this work sets the tone for much of his subsequent writing. He quotes the prophecy of Hosea (1:2): "The children of Judah and the children of Israel will be gathered together and will appoint for themselves one head and will go out from the land." In a typical interpretation he translates this into contemporary terms: "The beginning of the redemption will be that Israel will gather as a single organization and with a single resolve to appoint a leader and go up from the land, 'from the land of their dispersions' as Targum Onkelos describes it" (*op. cit.*, 200).

Alkalai continues that the first step is to appoint in every location God-fearing men of substance who possess initiative to direct everything pertaining to the ingathering (*op. cit.*, 200). He also stresses the need for funds to achieve redemption, which he regards as the mitzvah of tithing.

Alkalai had no illusions about how difficult it would be to convince the Jewish people of the necessity to return to its homeland. Drawing on quotes from Scripture and Talmudic texts, he mentions that redemption will come little by little.

> We are a stiff-necked people. Even among the children of Israel, after all their afflictions and the miracles they had witnessed, only one in five or one in fifty or one in five hundred wished to leave

Egypt, while those who did not died during the three days of darkness. How much more true this is at a time when we live at ease and peace in the lands of the nations. (*op. cit.,* 201 and 206)

He warned against the facile assumption that the steps he proposed would lead to the Messiah and the ultimate redemption. Such a concept would be similar to maintaining that daylight precedes sunrise. The redemption would come step by step. Its first stage would be the Josephian, or preparatory, messiah, who would ingather the exiles. This in turn would lead to the ultimate messiah, descendant from King David.

As part of this process, Alkalai emphasized the importance of grammar and the knowledge of each Hebrew word, together with the necessity of a common language, if the organization he proposed was to operate effectively. He pointed out that two parts of the Jewish world (Eastern Europe Ashkenazim and North African Sephardim) spoke the vernacular of the countries where they lived, which made communication difficult. However difficult, he considered the learning of Hebrew essential in order to create a common language (246–247).

A Call to the Jewish People

While Alkalai was attempting to spread his ideas for achieving redemption to the Jewish People, Europe was in a ferment stimulated by uprisings in 1848, which were intended to achieve political independence for the nations of the Continent. Alkalai's manifesto was a reply to his many opponents, who attacked his ideas sharply. Among his critics were not only rabbis who believed that redemption must come by direct Divine intervention, but also by the Jewish press, notably the *Orient,* which was published in Germany. The response of Ignatz Einhorn (1825–1875), a prominent Reform rabbi, was particularly bitter and derisive.

Alkalai's explanation that his proposals were meant to achieve the first stage of redemption rather than the final redemption, which would occur by Divine intervention, did not pacify his critics. One senses, not only in this manifesto but also in his other writings, that he was moved by the Damascus Affair, Jewish persecutions in general and by the wakening of nationalism in the Balkans at the time.

Minchat Yehudah is presented in two parts. In the first he sets out his interpretation of the word *teshuva* which, he points out, means both "repentance" and "return." In his typical use of homiletics, he connects both concepts with the obligation for Jews to return to the Land of Israel. The sources include Demaar and BT *Ketubbot* (110b) where it is stated that one who lives outside Eretz Israel is likened to one who has no God. He also cites Nachmanides, who considered the return to Eretz Israel an obligatory mitzvah.

In the second part of his work, he welcomed Montefiore's plan to build a workshop to train men in order to muster support for his idea of establishing Jewish settlements in Israel. He wrote that redemption would only be achieved by approaching the rulers of nations, and asked: "Is it not for our own nobility to undertake this task?" The task, he wrote, would begin in Great Britain.

What motivated Alkalai to choose Great Britain as the country most likely to support the return of the Jewish people to its homeland? An article in 1952 inexplicably advances the reason that it would be through Queen Victoria. It is more likely he was motivated by the intervention of Lord Palmerston, the British Foreign Secretary, in approaching the Turkish government to save the Jews of the Balkans. The involvement of Sir Moses Montefiore in the Yishuv may also have been a fator in his choice.

His prediction of the role that Great Britain would play in the redemption of the Jewish people was intended to appeal to the widest possible readership. Unlike his previous scholarly writings, in which he used long passages quoting from all parts of the Bible and the commentaries, his work, *Mevasser Tov,* which was translated into English as *Harbinger of Good Tidings* and published in 1852, is intended for a more general readership. In the summary of this work he writes, inter alia:

> to prove that by the sacred writings that we are commanded by the association of the whole nation to work out our return to the Holy Land. I have shown that this return and the building of the

Temple are independent of the advent of the Messiah and must take place before that event.... We must not attempt our return in a body by force of arms but by firmly obtaining the aid of the just and generous nations that have hitherto protected us. I have tried to dispel the idea that our return must be achieved by miraculous deeds.... Internal dissentions caused our ruin and unity and brotherhood alone will atone for that fault.... Union is strength.... The movement must originate with us....

He set out in some detail the necessary steps for accomplishing this purpose. First, it would be through the rulers, even though ultimate redemption comes from God alone. Second, "the heads of Diaspora Jewish communities must join forces and create a single organization that will obtain permission from the rulers for us to return to our ancestral inheritance."[2]

Visits to Western Europe

Alkalai was not content to rely entirely on his writings to stimulate the return to Eretz Israel. In 1851 he visited European capitals in order to present his ideas. In London he founded Shalom Yerushalaim, a society for settlement in Israel that disintegrated shortly after he left England. While in London he spoke to some leading personalities (there is no indication of their identities) about the idea of settling in Eretz Israel and reported as follows:

One person said, "We know the Jews are both rich and learned." Therefore, he had faith in our general treasury with all his soul.

Another leader said, "The gold of Australia has been discovered in our time on behalf of the Jews;" while still another said, 'There is in our treasury the great fund which one leader left for the ingathering of the exiles and when they begin to return, we will give it to them." Yet a fourth said, "That has been set aside for this holy purpose without any single deduction." These are the consoling words that my ears heard at that time.[3]

---

[2] Becketts, 1852. From the Gershon Sholem National Library, Jerusalem.
[3] Ha-rav Y.H. Alkalai amut Tel-Aviv, 26.

He founded similar societies in other European cities.

In 1852 he met Rabbi Dr. Yehiel Michael Sachs, one of Europe's outstanding intellects, in Berlin, then the capital of Prussia. Sachs received him particularly well because he was studying the poetry of the Spanish sages (Alkalai was, of course, a Sephardi). Impressed by Alkalai, Sachs called him "a Chacham (Torah scholar) of wide knowledge, with clarity of vision who is worthy of serious attention."[4]

During an 1857 visit to Western Europe, Alkalai published *Goral la-Adonai,* another treatise that outlined his ideas about redemption and the Land of Israel, in which he stressed once more the importance of tithing in order to support nascent settlements in Israel. *Goral la-Adonai,* which was probably the most popular of his writings, had an immediate impact all over Europe.

Alkalai paid his second visit to Germany in 1850, where he found receptive ears among leading rabbis and thinkers such as Jacob Ettlinger, Eliezer Horowitz, Zunz, Gedalia Titkin, Jellinek and others. It is significant that he was able to influence such men of diverse interests and beliefs. He distributed the imprimatur to *Goral la-Adonai,* but despite critical acclaim it appears to have had no influence.

He traveled widely to propagate his ideas and visited Breslau, Leipzig and Paris, among other cities. Among those he spoke to were Moses Montefiore, Adolph Cremieux, Karl Netter, Albert Cohen and members of the Rothschild family, and received several letters of recommendation that encouraged him.[5]

World Jewish Organizations

In 1861, Alkalai published a pamphlet entitled *Mashish shalom* about the proposal of Rabbi Ludwig Philipson (1811–1889) to establish an international organization, to be called Agudat Israel, which would unify Jewish communities. He also organized a gathering of leading Jewish figures in Paris with this purpose in mind. While the *Encyclopaedia Judaica*'s entry on religious Zionism mentions this work as referring to the

---

[4] Y. Gur Ari, *Op. cit.,* 25–26.
[5] *Op. cit.,* 27–28.

formation of the Alliance, the article's heading clearly specifies that it refers to the organization formed by Philipson.

We hear nothing more about the proposed organization. However, it is significant that Alkalai accepted Philipson's support for the proposal even though the latter was a Reform Jew. Alkalai's belief that all efforts to unify the Jewish people should be supported regardless of their provenance foreshadows similar policies on the part of Jacob Reines, the founder of Mizrachi. Reines joined the Zionist Organization despite fundamental differences with its leaders over matters of belief. Under his leadership, the Mizrachi became an integral part of the Zionist Organization and, in due course, partners with the government of the State of Israel.

The Origins of the Alliance Israélite Universelle

Philipson's fruitless attempt to unify the Jewish people reflected a deeply-felt need among leading Jews in Europe for an international organization to assist Jewish communities in all aspects of their lives, both internal and in relation to the world at large. This feeling crystallized in the formation of the Alliance Israélite Universelle in 1860, largely through the efforts of the French statesman, Adolphe Crémieux (1796–1880).

Sefer Chaim

In 1856, this, Alkalai's longest work in Hebrew (his earlier writings were in Ladino), was published in Belgrade. Like most of his longer writings, it is discursive, and makes reference to many ideas unrelated to his main theme of return and redemption. Some of them however, are of unusual interest and will be summarized below.

He first deals with the relationship between Israel and the nations, interpreting the verse "He will turn the heart of the parents to the children" (from the book of Malachi) to mean that "redemption will come through the kings of the earth, the kings of Edom and Ishmael." He continues that God will turn the hearts of the kings of the earth to their fathers because we are all the descendants of one human being and one God created us. "There is no doubting the spiritual superiority of the Jewish people." Finally, he quotes, "Strangers will tend your sheep and the descendants of foreigners will be your fathers.... But you will be God's priests" (Isaiah 61:5).

He then contrasts prophetic vision with Israel's current condition. "They [the nations] are elevated in qualities and their fellow Jews, who are devoted to serving the Creator of the world, are scattered and separated amongst the nations."[6]

Alkalai tried to explain why the rabbis of earlier generations failed to take steps to hasten the redemption, but like nearly all Orthodox rabbis of his time, he lacked historical perspective and could only suggest, "Perhaps they saw that their generations were not worthy of redemption and had not the strength." About his contemporaries, however, he said, "The kings of our generation are kings of kindness and mercy and lovers of righteousness."

He then mentions the second factor that distinguished his generation from previous generations: there were great personalities in the Jewish people who had access to contemporary rulers, whom he said would have a share in the World to Come.[7]

Alkalai makes brilliant use of homiletics to stress his social message. He quotes rabbinic and scriptural sources that point to the overwhelming spiritual superiority achieved by those who live in Eretz Israel over those who live in the Diaspora, and says that those who live in the Holy Land are forgiven their sins.

He also cites the Midrash that just as that angels from outside Israel do not enter the Eretz Israel and angels in Eretz Israel do not travel to the Diaspora, so too the souls of those who move from the Diaspora to the Land of Israel do not accompany them. As soon as they enter Eretz Israel, their "foreign" souls are exchanged for native ones, they are forgiven his sins and are spiritually reborn.[8]

In this work, Alkalai goes much further than exultation of the land of Israel. He quotes with approval Rabbi Kolen Yodan, who wrote, "If you place your children in the land, they will accept me as God, but if not,

---

[6] *Op. cit.,* 436–437.
[7] *Op. cit.,* 44.
[8] *Op. cit.,* 416.

they will not accept me as God."[9] He then draws several conclusions from the Shema (Deuteronomy 6:4–9 and Numbers 15:37–41, which observant Jews recite twice daily), some clearly implied, others as a result of exaggerated exegesis. In the first category, the tzitzit (ritual fringes) serve as a metaphor for the ingathering of the exiles from the four corners of the earth.

Alkalai cites the first verse of the Shema, "Hear, O Israel: the Lord our God, the Lord is One" as strong evidence that redemption depends on general return to the land. To explain this apparently strange conclusion, he says that people who return to Eretz Israel should be called by the name Israel because outside the land we are called by the name of Jacob. Moreover, God will be our God because one who lives outside the land is as one who has no God (BT *Ketubbot* 110b). Since one who lives outside Eretz Israel is as though he has no God, the verse addressed to Israel must therefore be addressed specifically to those who live in Eretz Israel.[10]

Alkalai then draws practical conclusions from the second paragraph of the Shema, which deals with the mitzvah of tefillin. Noting that tefillin are traditionally worn on the left hand, he cites the verse "In her left hand are riches and honor" (Proverbs 3:16) to show that the future redemption will come through the influential and wealthy Jews. It is unclear whether his interpretation of these passages led him to approach prominent figures like Cremieux and Montefiore for financial support of Jewish settlements in Israel or whether he did so as a practical course of action in order to help achieve the goal of returning to the land. If the second possibility is true, Alkalai may have quoted the relevant verses in order to enlist their support for the project.

Even in this mainly ideological book, Alkalai stresses the practical problems of settlement, financial support required by the Yishuv and the provision of work for those living there.

---

[9] *Op. cit.*, 465.
[10] *Op. cit.*, 514.

Rabbi Alkalai and the Alliance Israélite Universelle

Alkalai welcomed enthusiastically the founding of the Alliance in 1860. It seemed to meet all his proposals, particularly for the worldwide unity of the Jewish People and support for settlement in Israel. In his work *Bat Zion,* which was published in 1869, he wrote that through this organization, Jews from all over the world and its opposing denominations, Orthodox and Reform, could be brought together. It would put an end to false beliefs and, by the appointment of supervisors, would be able to end the divisions through "the written and the spoken word… until they make the people as one."[11] He also expected substantial help, financial and in training immigrants for settlement in Israel.

In one typical passage, he wrote: "Today the prophecy of Hosea that 'the sons of Judah and Israel shall be gathered together from the land' has been realized." In other words, because Israel would soon be gathered into one organization of the Alliance and they will have one leader (president). "This holy company will supervise matters of the ingathering, and its first result will be settlement in Eretz Israel," he wrote.

In this work he made practical proposals, again stressing the importance of tithing in order to support settlement, land purchases, the growing of crops, the planting of vineyards, the construction of homes, the development of crafts and the building of ships. He praised Montefiore and Lord Rothschild for their contributions to the development of the Yishuv.

However, Alkalai's hopes were unrealistic. Among the early members of the Alliance were Reform Jews, whom most Orthodox rabbis could not support even if they did not oppose the organization openly. In addition, while the group's aims included support for Jewish education, intervention to protect Jews from discrimination and persecution, providing financial assistance to Jews in poverty and fighting for emancipation, settlement in Israel was not considered one of the

---

[11] *Op. cit.,* 651–652.

organization's goals. No reference was made to Eretz Israel as a special sphere of its interest.

Besides, the practical work that the Alliance initiated or supported initially was not substantial in the eyes of Alkalai, who thought in terms of large-scale settlement in the land and of building of towns in the country. Nevertheless, in a letter to the Hebrew newspaper *Ha-magid* in 1869, he praised the Alliance for its help in settling Jews in the land and establishing an agricultural school, Mikve Yisrael. His contemporary, Zvi Hirsch Kalischer, kept in closer contact with the Alliance, but was also unable to persuade the organization to become involved in the settlement on a large scale. This changed to some extent after the founding of the World Zionist Organization in 1897.

Meoded Anavim

In a long discourse published in Jerusalem in 1864, Alkalai returned to some of the themes he had explored over the previous fifteen years. There may have been signs of despair over the possibility of achieving the aims he had set out in previous writings, especially as he had stressed the importance of action by the Jews who settled in Eretz Israel as the first steps to redemption – a view that was anathema to most Orthodox rabbis and many Orthodox laymen. He quotes Rabbenu Bachya, who wrote, "Human beings should do all they can by natural means. What nature lacks, miracles will supply." Alkalai adds, "What Israel begins (and the beginning is to make a general request on behalf of our people to the world leaders), God will conclude by inclining their hearts to grant the request."[12]

This is another way of making his original point that the beginning of redemption will come by the actions of the Jewish people through the Messiah son of Joseph rather than through divine intervention. The ultimate redemption will come directly from God through the Messiah son of David. He later addresses the same idea when he contemplates two stages in redemption: the ingathering of the exiles and the subsequent building of the Temple.[13]

---

[12] *Op. cit.*, 3.
[13] *Op. cit.*, 956.

Although Alkalai had expressed these opinions in earlier writings, he did not do so with the sharpness of the current example. For example, he used halachic language to suggest that Jews would not be permitted to establish new cities and settlements in the land of Israel without the acquiescence of the nations of the world. "*We may not* do so except by permission of the rulers of the land.... They will... proclaim freedom to return to our land and to our ancestral inheritance."[14]

He reiterates that salvation will come with the agreement of the non-Jewish rulers of the land, citing the precedent of Ezra and Nehemia, who obtained permission from Cyrus, King of Persia, to resettle the land in 537 B.C.E.[15]

As always, Alkalai comments on some practical matters. He urged Jews to build houses even if they did not live in them. If they could not be sold privately, they should be up for sale by auction (a suggestion with contemporary echoes).[16]

He felt that the descriptions "Ashkenazim" and "Sephardim" should be phased out of the vernacular and replaced by "Yisraelim" – Jews. He also felt that all Jews should speak Hebrew. At present, he said, we are scattered amongst seventy nations and speak seventy languages. Therefore we must have one language which must be spoken in our Holy Land.

To support this notion, he quotes in Rashi on the verse, "You shall teach them to your children and talk of them" (Deuteronomy 11:19). He said that this means that Jews everywhere are commanded to teach their children to speak in the Holy Tongue.[17]

Surprisingly, Alkalai stresses that the first stage of redemption must come from the Jewish people without expectation of heavenly assistance. "The beginning of the redemption will come from the people itself, with God's help... and the end of the redemption will come through the Great Redeemer, the Messiah of the House of David."[18] He also stresses

---

[14] *Op. cit.,* 617.
[15] *Op. cit.,* 623.
[16] *Op. cit.,* 609.
[17] *Op. cit.,* 610.
[18] *Op. cit.,* 623.

again that salvation will come by reference to the rulers of the land, referring specifically to the precedent of Ezra and Nehemia, who obtained permission from Cyrus, the King of Persia to resettle the land in 537 B.C.E.

Significantly, Alkalai also declares that this must not detract from Maimonides's assertion that all events that affect individuals and nations are miracles and outside the natural realm. He tries to overcome this difficulty by saying that the first stage of redemption will be a hidden miracle (presumably he is saying it is a miracle, but a natural one, in keeping with Maimonides's opinion).

Alkalai and Reform

An essay entitled "Kibbutz Galuyot," written in 1869, illustrates clearly his views on Reform Judaism. Although he completely rejects the theological basis of non-halachic Judaism, as might be expected, his tone is surprisingly moderate and reflects the supreme importance he attached to the unity of the Jewish people.

He criticized the Reform movement severely for introducing innovations to the form of prayers modeled on general forms of worship, omitting reference to Jerusalem and to David's kingdom and the gathering of the exiles. He believed that this development occurred because the people despaired of redemption during the long exile.

He wrote that the Jewish people contains two diametrically opposed sub-nations, "lovers of freedom and haters of freedom." He said there were lovers and haters of the new, with one side of the battle fighting in the name of Torah, the other in the name of secular knowledge. "The lovers of freedom," he wrote, "vote for freedom of thought to break free of the yoke of Torah and the mitzvot and the yoke of the Kingdom of Heaven."

He then named the Alliance as the body that could unite both sides. In that case, he said, "We would be one people with one heart, one society, one language, one Torah, one set of customs – the customs of Israel."[19]

---

[19] *Op. cit.,* 603–605.

This hope was unrealistic due to the bitterness that had developed between Orthodox and Reform groups. While at one stage a compromise might have been possible, the opposition of Hungarian Orthodoxy, the strongest Orthodoxy in central Europe under the leadership of Rabbi Moses Sofer (known as the Chatam Sofer [1762–1839]), made such an arrangement impossible. Sofer was implacably opposed to any kind of accommodation with the Reform movement even though some of its adherents did not desire a complete break with traditional Jewish practice.[20]

This essay gives us a rare glimpse into Alkalai's character. He thanks the Alliance for "recognizing me as a man of stature and honoring me with the letter that Minister Cremieux signed," and there is a refreshing naivety in the words that one cannot help but find endearing. He expresses gratitude and praise for Rabbi Kalischer's essay, "The Welfare of Jerusalem," which had become an influential work throughout Europe. In general, Alkalai venerated Kalischer, upon whom he bestowed high praise on the latter's seventieth birthday in 1865.

Alkalai and Problems of the Yishuv

In his 1886 article, "Mevasser Tov," Alkalai wrote that problems in the Yishuv – crushing poverty and the first internal tensions in Jerusalem – could only be solved if the divisions within its population ended. Everything had to be achieved by the community as a whole. He specifically opposed individual initiatives that did not include the entire Yishuv. In a specific reference to one Dr. Furst, who chartered a ship to take deliveries to Palestine, Alkalai ascribed the project's failure to the fact that this was a private initiative. "The spirit of the time does not ask of each individual to proceed as he wishes," he wrote, "but demands the strength of the entire community."[21]

Instead, Alkalai set out proposals to improve conditions in the country – the construction of homes either for veteran residents or in order to make rentals available for new immigrants, with the help of loans if necessary. In his view, rents from these properties could be used to

---

[20] *Ibid.*
[21] *Op. cit.,* 696.

support the poor, enabling them to rent their own accommodations. He maintained that such land-development projects were a mitzvah, which he derived from God's command to Adam to care for the Garden of Eden, and believed that they would be the foundation of the Yishuv. His approach to the building of Israel foreshadowed the insistence of Aaron David Gordon (1856–1922) on labor as the foundation of the country. Alkalai differed with the secular Gordon, who sought to create a "religion of labor," preferring the opposite construction: religion through labor.

Alkalai's proposals were vigorously opposed by those who raised funds from abroad for distribution to the poor, particularly for religious communities who wished to spend their lives immersed in Torah learning. These groups feared that their fundraising efforts would suffer if money were to be invested in settling the land. The pleas of Alkalai and of Kalischer that developing the land would also provide sustenance for students of Torah were of no avail.[22]

Alkalai and the Yishuv

Alkalai did not allow exaggeration of the hardships in Eretz Israel to pass without comment. He replied to advice given in the periodical *Ha-levanon* warning potential immigrants of severe hardships in Eretz Israel and advising them not to immigrate because "it is better to die by the sword than through hunger," and he disputed the exaggerated picture of poverty in the land, pointing out "God did not say the houses would be silver and gold". No one died of hunger (*op. cit.,* 694).

To this point, Alkalai's insistence of the redemptive power of settlement in Israel was not the reflection of personal experience in the land itself. In 1871, he went there to investigate, in order to report upon his return about the need "to awaken the hearts of our great leaders, to establish colonies and settle our Holy Land"[23] In a letter, dated 26 Adar, 1871, Alkalai criticizes those who opposed settling the land and quotes at some length Kalischer's essay, "A Voice on the Water," in which the author describes an approach made to the Sultan (Palestine being under

---

[22] See Kretl, Rabbi Alkalai and Z.H. Kalischer. Youth Department of the Zionist Executive, 28.)

[23] Article on Alkalai, *The Encyclopedia of Religious Zionism,* VOl. 1, 138.

Turkish rule) which resulted in permission for Jews to purchase lands and vineyards. This letter reflects his ideas and reactions to what he experienced.

Alkalai went so far as to say that building the land would result in reconciliation between Jews and non-Jews, adding a rather unrealistic warning that if the Jews did not go there, "many powerful nations would come to the land in order to be God's people" (based on Zachariah, Chapter 22). Alkalai then listed the names of all those who opposed settlements in Eretz Israel, but they do not appear in the article as finally printed, since they were deleted by the censor.[24]

Visit to Eretz Israel

During a visit to Israel, Alkalai approached the Rishon le-Zion, Rabbi Yehudah Halevy, and other Sephardi notables, who promised their assistance if the Ashkenazim would join them. Some members of the Ashkenazi community, including Rabbi Shlomo Hazan, also promised support. Although a joint meeting was arranged, it did not take place.

However, Alkalai was not easily discouraged. He was able to arrange a joint meeting of Sephardim and Ashkenazim after private meetings with representatives of each rabbinate. The group agreed to form a society to be called "All Israel Are Brothers" that would support settling the land in order to provide a living for the poor.

Alkalai also suffered a great deal of derision and condemnation, particularly from Rabbi Akiva Lehren (1795–1876) of Amsterdam, who said it was a sin to base hopes for redemption on working the land. Redemption, he said, would not come until the whole land had repented.

Lehren's opposition led rabbis in Jerusalem to boycott the All Israel Are Brothers society, and at a meeting of the heads of the Yishuv in Jerusalem a resolution passed calling on magazines and newspapers not to accept any articles by Alkalai relating to Eretz Israel.[25] Alkalai responded fiercely to these attacks, saying that opposition to his work would "destroy our land and end our peace." He promised that he would neither "keep silent nor exercise restraint… until his opponents admit

---

[24] *Op. cit.,* 714–717.
[25] *Ha-levanon* 8/28: 220, quoted by Kresel, Rabbi Y. Alkalai and Z.H. Kalischer, 29–30.

their sin in the wrong they had done to the Holy Land [and] cease to clothe themselves in pretended piety and self-righteousness in a lying cause."[26] In a particularly sharp statement, he wrote, "Who knows what has separated and distanced Israel from their Father in Heaven? [It is] the *zedim* [wicked ones] who prefer evil to good, falsity to righteousness, who profane the Torah and those who learn it and slander the good land and those who love it in order to make the land hated in the eyes of our people."[27]

Furthermore, in a letter to *Ha-Magid,* Alkalai describes graphically the opposition to his new society, where members would not be described as Sephardim or Ashkenazim but rather as Israelites. Describing the toast that marked the formation of the new society, he wrote:

> My heart was joyous when I heard via *Ha-havazelet* that the government intended to sell to the Alliance a large tract of land, which Mr. Netter will supervise, at a reduced price. How sad that some Ashkenazi rabbis in Jerusalem oppose our society with all their might. Rabbi Fischel had to leave the society as a result of their opposition.... In their eyes, settlement in Eretz Israel and sustenance from work and labor in the land of Zion is like a painful thorn.... The Rishon le-Zion asked me not to enter into a dispute in Eretz Israel because of his reputation.... For months since my return [to Serbia] I have not said a word.... My consolation is to see the Society in Jerusalem grow bigger and bigger.[28]

Although Alkalai was sometimes slow to respond harshly to his opponents and rarely used intemperate language, there were exceptions. In a letter to Rabbi Akiva Leran, who spoke disparagingly about the Society, Alkalai sarcastically asked, "Is this the man who curses, the man for whom the honor of the Torah and those who learn it is as dear to him as the apple of his eye? This is nothing but a slander.... First of all,

---

26 *Ha-havazelet.*
27 "B'nei Yisrael." *Ha-magid* 3 (1872): 25).
28 *Ha-magid,* 1872.

he should have asked about the nature of the Society, who its members and founders are."

He called on the Rishon le-Zion to inform Rabbi Lehren of the merits of the Society. At the end of the letter, he quoted the Talmudic dictum that "all beginnings are difficult" in order to encourage those who worked for the settlement of Eretz Israel.

Nevertheless, Alkalai continued to suffer from unrestrained attacks. In a letter to Havazelet in 1872, he refers again to the rabbis who wrote derogatory comments about the Society to the Beth Din. He apparently feared that such remarks might have a negative effect outside the country because in this letter he remarked that Kalischer had received good advice to visit the country and to see for himself.

His fears were not unfounded. Despite the Society's initial success in recruiting members, constant attacks from communal leaders led several rabbis in Eretz Israel who had previously assisted in his work to withdraw their support. Presumably as a result of this, the Society was dissolved shortly after he left the country.

Relationship with Kalischer

From *Ha-havazelet* we can see a reflection of the relationship between Alkalai and Kalischer. In a letter to the former, Kalischer refers to him with the effusive title "*Ha-gaon ha-zaddik*" (the righteous genius), and continues to report that one Rabbi Mamberger of Wurzberg wished to send two supervisors to oversee arrangements for kosher food in the settlements. It is interesting that Alkalai's reaction to this proposal was that two supervisors would not be enough. He believed the settlements would require the presence of the greatest scholars in the application of halacha.

Alkalai's opponents were not satisfied and continued their attacks on him, even stooping to forgery in order to discredit him. In a letter to *Ivri anochi* in 1873, Alkalai refers to one such forgery, reportedly from one Rabbi Akiva, in which the author referred to his Society as a bunch of farmers and workers of the land (then considered to be plebeians of society). Alkalai took pains to praise the Society's members as righteous people (tzaddikim) and the elders of society. The exchange is an interesting reflection of society in the country at that time.[29]

Also from that year there are letters related to the Jews of Romania, who were suffering from severe persecution and for whom immigration to the United States was suggested. Alkalai, like Kalischer, vigorously opposed the idea, insisting that they should be absorbed into the Yishuv. He wrote a letter addressed to the Alliance suggesting they send a representative to the Sultan of Turkey in the name of the Jewish people, in order to buy land for settling for Romanian Jews there.[30] Anticipating opposition to this proposal on the grounds that the country could not absorb them, Alkalai pointed out in another letter that near the country were cities through which trade passed. Also, the completion of the Suez Canal in 1869 allowed for the passage of goods (presumably, he considered Eretz Israel would benefit from this development).[31]

The same year, he wrote again to *Ivri anochi,* this time to say the group was founded by God to oversee the ingathering of the exiles.

Immigration to Israel

In 1873 Alkalai immigrated to Israel, where he spent the last five years of his life. There is no record of any considerable correspondence or activity during that period. Advancing age and the many journeys he had made as a younger man in the cause of settlement had taken their toll. However, his letters from this period provide a window into his personality and the conditions in the Yishuv at the time.

The first of these letters appeared in *Ha-havazelet,* congratulating the paper on what was written regarding settlement of the land and crafts.[32] He quoted the Book of Psalms (16:9), "my heart rejoiced and my honor was glad," and continued:

> I was honored to be a guest [of the Alliance – R.G.] at Mikve Israel because the prestigious community honored me with

---

[29] See the *Encyclopedia of Religious Zionism,* 139, for more information.
[30] *Ivri anochi* 9/6.
[31] *Ivri anochi* 9/13 (1872) quoted in the writings of Y. Alkalai, Y. Rafael, and A.I. Kook, 1974, 743–745.
[32] *Ha-havazelet* 5/16 (1875)

applause and thanks. This great honor is to me a sign that God has approved my work, and my prediction came true that those who opposed me will be "like chaff before the wind" [Psalms 35:5].

He praised communities in London for their intention to found colonies and settle the land, and said the Polish Jewish community was shrinking as the Jews from the continent continued to settle in Israel.[33] His letter shows an innocence and modesty that are incongruous when we compare them to the consistent firmness and faith with which he had expressed his ideas over the years.

The following year he wrote to *Ha-havazelet,* praising the communities that had decided on a project (unfortunately not completed) to honour Moses Montefiore for his efforts with the Sultan concerning settlements in the land. Always practical – when not overwhelmed by his own enthusiasm – he called for the reconstruction of a workshop for the manufacture of material from the plant of the cotton family that Montefiore had established twenty years before. The workshop had failed because its managers had never seen that kind of manufacturing, with the result that not only did the work cease, but the workshop and machinery became worthless. Restoring the factory would not only provide employment for hundreds of people, and expert craftsmen in this field were brought into the country to train them.

It appears from this letter that Rothschild was an advisor of the Turkish Sultan from whom Alkalai felt that they must ask permission to buy land "which is the inheritance of our ancestors." He called for unity with the Alliance and was confident that the Sultan would not turn them away "because he loves kindness and loves righteousness and law" (references to Micah 7:18 and Psalms 33:5 respectively). In words that have an obsequious ring to modern ears he added, "It is well known to our lord the Sultan that the Jews are faithful servants… of his kingdom, and he in his love and mercy will treat us according to his abundant mercy because we have been sated with shame for eighteen hundred years."

---

[33] *Op. cit.,* 758–759.

When doubts were expressed as to whether a large-scale immigration of the thirty thousand Jews in Persia would be practicable, Alkalai pointed out that the majority were farmers, although some were artisans. He said that the large numbers of the proposed project should not intimidate leaders of the Yishuv since the immigrants would not arrive en masse but rather little by little – a favorite phrase of Alkalai's – until homes were constructed for them.

In the last recorded letter (*Ha-havazelet* 6/43 [1876]), there is an interesting indication of the conditions in Eretz Israel at the time. Alkalai objected to the visit of Lord Montagu,[34] who wished to see for himself "the land's plagues and deficiencies: the thing is known and it is known that the land is desolate and ruined, and is given over to the hands of desolate men who sanctify and exalt its desolation and shame anyone who wishes to sell it" (a clear reference to those who did not work but rather lived on charity and opposed settling the land – R.G.).

Alkalai added bitterly that unity among the ethnic groups would not be achieved "because there is no cure for hatred that stems from envy." Any agent sent to represent organizations from abroad in connection with settlements would "not be able to bear the evils and slanders they would publish about him."

These words sum up all that had been achieved over the previous thirty-five years: a sad epilogue for a man who throughout his life had urged settlement of Eretz Israel as the supreme task of the Jewish people.

---

[34] Probably a reference to the visit on behalf of The Sir Moses Montefiore Testimonial Fund in 1874 to promote agriculture and other industrial occupations (The diaries of Sir Moses and Lady Judith Montefiore. The Jewish Historical Society in England, 1983, 164–165).

Rabbi Zvi Hirsch Kalischer   הרב צבי הירש קלישר

RABBI ZVI HIRSCH KALISCHER
(1795–1874)

ZVI HIRSCH KALISCHER was the son of a distinguished rabbinical family who traced their ancestry back to Rabbi Judah Loew of Prague (known as the Maharal, 1525–1609). He was borne in Lissa, an important center of Jewish learning in what is now Poland, which was known for being open to Western culture.

This environment left its mark on Kalischer. In his younger days he learned with his uncle Yehudah Leib Kalischer, who was the head of the rabbinical court in Lithuania, where the primary sources of his learning lay in Jacob Ba'al ha-Havat Da'at and Akiva Eger of Posen (1761–1837). As might have been anticipated from the intellectual interests typical of the town, his studies included Kabbala (Jewish mysticism), Jewish philosophy of the Middle Ages (a particularly unusual discipline for a traditional rabbi at that time), Descartes, Spinoza, Mendelssohn and Kant.

In addition to traditional Torah learning and the study of philosophy, Kalischer also read the emerging Hebrew literature of the day, including that of the *Haskalah*, the Jewish enlightenment movement. It is surprising that in spite of his interest in philosophy and Western thought, Kalischer was not free of medieval superstition. For example, he believed strongly in the efficacy of charms used by his mentor, Rabbi Akiva Eger, which he recommended as a protection against the plague which had broken out in the city of Lasloy.[1]

After his marriage, Kalischer moved from Lissa to Thorn, where in spite of his initial reluctance to take on the position, he became the

---

[1] Gur-Arieh, Yitzchak. *Kalischer*, 27–29.

community rabbi, remaining in the post for fifty years. Although his efforts to persuade the Jewish people to return to Eretz Israel involved frequent fundraising trips around Europe, writing articles, considerable correspondence with other rabbis and leading personalities in Europe and the publication of his book *Derishat Zion* (Yearning for Zion, 1862), he appears to have been a caring and effective rabbi of his local community.

Major Works

The keys to Kalischer's thought and life's work lay in *Derishat Zion* and *Emunah Yeshara* (Honest Faith, 1843). It is therefore essential to summarize their main themes as a preface to this essay.

Although the earlier of these two writings, *Emunah Yeshara,* was written in 1843 and not published until many years later, it was in effect Kalischer's encounter with philosophy, secular-religious tension and particularly the relationship between faith and reason. He opposed the idea that religion could only be preserved through logic, although he ascribed

> ...great benefit... if he [the reader – R.G.] researches... to the point that intellect can reach in order to understand the roots of religion and faith.... On the other hand, the researcher who says, "I will not believe anything until my intellect understands it," will not achieve faith and will never be in the community of the righteous, because God's religion is beyond human comprehension.

In a clear echo of the medieval Yehudah Halevi, he states, "The basis of faith must rest on belief in 'signs and wonders.'" In the same work, Kalischer discusses and rejects philosophers such as Aristotle, Plato, Kant and Spinoza, but relies heavily on classic Jewish thinkers of the Middle Ages including Maimonides, Nachmanides, Albo and Arama. It is clear Kalischer was entirely bound by the traditional faith of Judaism to which philosophy remains the hand-maiden; philosophy in other words must not be independent; Kierkegaard's "leap of faith" has to be made.

Derishat Zion

Derishat Zion is rightly considered Kalischer's major work and is the key to his thought and subsequent writing. The book consists of four essays dealing with the ideological basis of his thought and with practical matters relating to settlement in the Land of Israel.

The purpose of the work is to "strengthen faith," since "because of our many sins, the number of hearts truly seeking God via his statutes and laws has declined."[2] Kalischer then deals with the nature of the relationship between faith and science.

First Essay, Part 1

In the first essay, he urges leaders of the Jewish community to take the initiative to form a capitalistic society for the settlement of Eretz Israel, and said that the land must be worked to produce its fruits. Kalischer believed the ingathering of the exiles was the prelude to the rebuilding of the Temple and the reinstitution of the Biblical sacrifices, and the ultimate fulfillment of the prophecies of Isaiah and Ezekiel.

He then deals with the process of redemption, and sets out his main theme; namely, that human effort is central to achieving the ultimate Messiah:

> Do not think that God will suddenly send the Messiah from Heaven to blow the great Shofar to the scattered people of Israel and gather them to Jerusalem (as promised through His servants the prophets).... Certainly all the words of the prophets will come to pass at the end of days, but not suddenly in one day. Rather, the redemption of Israel will come very slowly. The dawn of salvation will flower when Israel acts with courage... and realizes all the aims and promises of the holy prophets.[3]

Kalischer then addressed the question whether *teshuva,* usually translated as "repentance," is a necessary prerequisite for redemption. The prevailing view among rabbis at this time was that Divine

---

[2] Part 1, 8.
[3] Fishman, Zvi Hirsh Kalischer, Mosad Ha'Rav Kook, 60.

redemption would not come before the Jewish people repented of their sins, but Kalischer maintained strongly that while the beginning of the redemptive process does not depend on the Jews' repentance (*teshuva*), it nevertheless depends on *shuva* – return to the Land of Israel. It is interesting to note that even though there was little personal contact between Kalischer and Yehudah Alkalai, who was a contemporary of his, the ideology of both men was virtually identical.

First Essay, Part 2

Kalischer asks rhetorically whether the whole universe has been created without any purpose, then quotes liberally from Scripture, namely the prophets and writings, in order to support his view that salvation will commence through human efforts. "It is a great test for those who take part in this holy work… and go up to the desolate Land of Israel," he writes. "He who has the courage to do this will bring the redemption close."

He then expressed the unusual view that the persecutions that the Jewish People suffer in the Diaspora are comparable to those God used to test the ancient Israelites in the desert in Biblical.

Second Essay

The second section of *Derishat Zion* is devoted to a description of Israel and its importance, as described in the Tanach and the writings of the rabbis. He quotes the Talmudic passage (*Ketubbot* 110b) in which the rabbis say one who lives in Eretz Israel is like one who has a God, while one who lives outside Eretz Israel is like one who has no God. He also cites the prophet Isaiah, who claims that those who live in Eretz Israel are forgiven their sins.

Kalischer then quotes one of his mentors, Rabbi Yaakov Emden (1697–1776), who goes so far as to say that Jewish suffering over the centuries was a punishment for not living in their land. In even stronger support of that view, he refers to the work *Shevilei emunah* (Paths of

Faith), which maintains that when observant Jews live and worship in Eretz Israel, God will hear their prayers and bring the redemption.[4]

Addressing the objection that for centuries Jews had failed to settle in Israel in large numbers, he pointed out that previously Jews had neither the means nor the influence that would have made large-scale immigration possible, while in his generation most Jews were free and had produced leaders who were not public figures. The Jews, he wrote, should therefore take the courageous step to establish a society to develop and settle the country.[5]

Third Essay

In this part of his work, Kalischer deals with the restoration of the sacrificial service in the Temple. He believed this issue was of prime importance as part of the redemptive process leading to the Messiah of the House of David. He corresponded with leading halachic authorities of the generation, including Akiva Eger and Moshe Sofer, about the permissibility of sacrificial worship before the advent of the ultimate Messiah. These rabbis expressed the view that pending the arrival of the Messiah of the House of David, only the Passover sacrifice could be bought, but forbade sacrifices by individuals.

In the second part of this essay, Kalischer introduced a new subject unrelated to the sacrifices: a working plan for a new organization to the called The Society for Settling the Land. He lists four requirements to be met if any attempted settlement were to be successful. In order, they are:

1. Land purchase
2. Immigration from Russia, Poland and Germany should be encouraged and financial help provided until the land became profitable
3. Trained, armed guards must be trained for defense
4. The establishment of an agricultural school.

---

[4] *Op. cit.,* 67–68.
[5] *Op. cit.,* 69.

Kalischer stressed that the Society must be organized by "men who possess great political influence or finance."[6]

Kalischer and Moses Hess

Two years after the publication of *Derishat Zion,* Moses Hess (1812–1875) published his classic work, *Rome and Jerusalem,* which became one of the ideological foundations of secular Zionism. Hess came from an Orthodox family but rejected Judaism, partly as a result of his anthropological studies and partly due to influences from the emergence of liberation movements within the Austro-Hungarian Empire.

He concluded that the Jews, having preserved their nationality in exile, must now work for a political restoration in which those traditions would have an important role. He was also no doubt considerably influenced by the anti-Semitism in Europe and the fact that conversion to Christianity considered as a possible solution of the Jewish question, was powerless to stem. Delighted to hear that a prominent rabbi supported the concept of the return of the Jewish people to its ancient homeland, he wrote to Kalischer, "On the mountains of Mevasseret Jerusalem are the footsteps of the Great Society… which will awaken to the call of a rabbi who loves his people to bring to practical fruition the holy idea to restore devastated cities, to revive the earth from its desolation through Jewish workers under the protection of the great governments of the West."[7]

Kalischer wrote an addition to *Derishat Zion* called *Shelom Yerushalayim* (The Welfare of Jerusalem), to which Rabbi Eliyahu Gutmacher, the rabbi of Greditz, added a commentary. He described the relationship between the Jewish people, the Land of Israel and the Torah as a threefold thread that constitutes a single body. He added that even those who only supported the settlement of the land financially still acquired the merit of carrying out mitzvot based in the land as if they had settled there themselves. He also stressed that one should live in Israel in order

---

[6] Klausner, *The Zionist Writings of Zvi Kalischer.* Jerusalem: Mossad ha-Rav Kook, 45–46, 98–100.
[7] See Gur, Alkalai and Kalischer, 69–71, and Isaiah Berlin, Moses Hess.

to build it up rather than on the basis of receiving personal and financial support.[8]

Although the basis of Kalischer's ideas lay in Jewish sources with no reference to contemporary events, the influence of the rise of nationalism in Europe is evident in passages in *Derishat Zion* and his letters. In the former he writes, "This will be the object of praise and glory in the eyes of the nations, who will say that the Children of Israel are people with the spirit to demand and renew the inheritance of their Father. If the Italians and other peoples sacrifice themselves on behalf of their ancestral homeland, how much more so a land like this [*sic*], which all the world regards as holy while we stand afar, like a man who has no courage or heart."[9]

Even more graphically, Kalischer wrote in the German periodical *The Israelite* (No. 27, 1863): "We have enough examples of how other nations give of their possessions and their blood to recover land which was long lost to them. No sacrifice was too great to achieve their purpose. How much more for us Jews, whose nationhood is so strongly connected to our holy religion – should we fail in comparison with other nations?"[10]

Rabbinical Response to *Derishat Zion*

Although Moses Hess's enthusiastic endorsement of Kalischer's ideas was helpful, Kalischer was most concerned with how the rabbis of Central Europe would receive the work, and indeed, their reception was mixed.

Rabbi Samson Raphael Hirsch (1808–1888), the leader of the Orthodox community in Frankfurt-on-Main, author of an important commentary on the Torah and pioneer of the concept of Torah and Derech Eretz. While Hirsch supported settlers in Eretz Israel, he objected in principle to a movement whose inspiration was the desire to hasten the coming of the Messiah, which he believed would occur only by Divine intervention. Kalischer wrote to enlist his support, but after he failed to receive an answer, in 1862 he asked British Chief Rabbi Nathan

---

[8] *Encyclopedia of Religious Zionism*
[9] Federbush, *Chazon, Torah, Zion.* Mossad ha-Rav Kook, 40.
[10] Federbush, *Op. cit.,* 40.

Adler to approach Hirsch with a view towards changing the latter's mind. We have no record that anything resulted from this letter.

At around the same time, Kalischer also wrote to Rabbi Chaim Silverman of Patzk, but the result was the same.[11]

In addition to rabbis Hirsch and Silverman, Kalischer approached Rabbi Eliyahu Gutmacher, the rabbi of Greditz, an outstanding Talmudic scholar and charismatic figure and a student of Akiva Eger. Gutmacher was ambivalent about the stress on settlement, despite being a student of the great Akiva Eger, who had strongly supported the movement for a return to Eretz Israel and from whom therefore Kalischer might have expected unqualified support. Gutmacher believed that the return to the Land of Israel was a necessary component of the redemption process, and he initially wrote in terms similar to Kalischer to support the return to Eretz Israel in order to begin the task of "rousing the land from its slumber" and "to carry out such mitzvot as are possible at this time."[12] However, Gutmacher was nevertheless influenced by fierce opposition of many outstanding rabbis and Abraham Klausner (1874-1958, literary critic, historian and Zionist) wrote to him sharply in 1868 that he regarded those who denied his ideas as "denying prophecy."

Kalischer responded to his critics by citing the story of Gog and Magog (Ezekiel 3:39), which predicts the eventual return of Israel from all other lands to the Land of Israel, where they would all live securely, only to have that state of bliss shattered by a terrible war, followed by the arrival of the Messiah of the House of David. He asked: "How can we say that the Messiah will come suddenly?"

He also quoted the words recited at the end of the Passover Haggadah, "Next year in Jerusalem," to support his imperative for creating the conditions that would bring the ultimate Messiah. He believed these words express an instruction for the Jewish people first to return from exile; otherwise, the phrase would have been "May the Messiah of the House of David reign over us next year." However, the same phrase was cited by opponents as proof that Israel must wait

---

[11] *The Writings of Z.H. Kalischer.* Mossad ha-Rav Kook, 183, 185, 280.
[12] Chazon, *Torah ve-Zion.* Mossad ha-Rav Kook, 38.

passively for the Messiah to come. It appears that the words can be interpreted in either way.

Another prominent personality who opposed Kalischer's ideas was Rabbi Meir Auerbach, the head of the Ashkenazic rabbinic court in Jerusalem, who disputed the thesis that resettlement of Eretz Israel per se was a step towards redemption. First, he said, the Jewish People must repent in order to arouse love of Torah and attachment to the land – "the love of Zion and Jerusalem" as he put it.

Although Auerbach did not oppose settling the land, he saw practical difficulties in doing so. Kalischer replied that is was unrealistic to require repentance of the whole people as a prerequisite of the first stage towards redemption – namely, the re-settlement of Eretz Israel. He quoted a passage from the Zohar that says if a single group of settlers in the land did complete *teshuva,* God would consider it as if the whole nation had repented.[13]

On the political level, Auerbach was also skeptical about the possibility of obtaining international support for Kalischer's proposals through the influence of prominent Jews. He pointed out that in the fifteenth century, Don Isaac Abarbanel (1437–1508), was unable to prevent the expulsion of the Jews in 1492 despite his position as adviser to Ferdinand and Isabella, the king and queen of Spain. Similarly, he said, it would not be possible to obtain help from the Sultan of Turkey.

Kalischer replied that there was no analogy. Abarbanel, however, eminent, was alone and had to contend with a hostile and powerful Catholic Church, whereas prominent nineteenth-century Jews such as Montefiore and Cremieux had considerable influence in government circles.[14]

Rabbinic Support

Rabbinic supporters of Kalischer's ideas were in the minority. Most of the great religious leaders in Eastern Europe were adamantly opposed to the concept of immigration to Eretz Israel as a first step towards the Messianic era.

---

13 *The Writings of Rabbi Kalischer,* 199–202.
14 *Ibid.,* 200–201.

Rabbi Azriel Hildesheimer of Berlin (1820–1899), however, one of the outstanding protagonists of Hirsch's Torah and Derech Eretz ideology, enthusiastically supported Kalischer's ideas and when the Berlin Committee for settling Jews in Eretz Israel was in danger of collapse, he breathed new life into it. He had plans for new settlements but lacked the money they required.

Kalischer drew the greatest support for his ideas from Rabbi Yehudah Alkalai, an outstanding contemporary of his whose plans for the resettlement of Jews in Eretz Israel were strikingly similar to Kalischer's own writings. There appears to have been no contact between the two until Alkalai received a copy of *Derishat Zion* in 1863. In his essay *Meoded ha-anavim* (Encouragement for the Humble), published the following year, Alkalai included a defense of Kalischer's ideas.

Another rabbi to support Kalischer was Nathan Friedlander of Turigan, Latvia, who had written a book expressing ideas similar to those of Kalischer and approached the latter for an approbation, which Kalischer gladly gave him. Friedlander was also acquainted with Albert Cohen, who was in charge of the distribution of money to charities of Rothschild family and was interested in encouraging settlement in the Land of Israel. On receiving a friendly reaction from Cohen, he sent him a copy of *Derishat Zion* and suggested Kalischer write to Cohen, who had already established a hospital in Rothschild's name and a crafts school in Eretz Israel. Kalischer made contact and asked Cohen to persuade Rothschild to buy land in Eretz Israel and to approach Napoleon III, who was well-known as a supporter of national movements in Italy and Austria, for political support. The request received no response.

Rabbi Joseph Natonek of Hungary (1813–1892), received news of the founding of the Society for the Settlement of Eretz Israel with enthusiasm. He knew European languages and was able to enlist support. "Love of the Land of Israel burns like a fire in his heart," Kalischer wrote. Natonek dreamt of mass immigration to the country, of world-wide dissemination of the idea and also of approaching the Sultan. Despite his idealism, Kalischer was not impressed with what he regarded as impractical proposals and asked Natonek only to get authority for the purchase of land from the Turkish authorities. Despite protracted negotiations, Natonek's proposals bore no fruit. Kalischer's skepticism was justified. In light of subsequent history, Natonek's apparently unrealistic proposals were prophetic of the ideas that motivated and were expressed by Herzl.[15]

Problems of Settling the Land

For Kalischer, the skeleton of a plan to establish new settlements and provide proof-texts to show the importance of carrying out this work was one thing, and convincing skeptics of its practicality and ideological opponents that it was consistent with traditional Jewish teachings was quite another. The latter were fierce in their condemnation of the suggestion that human actions should be the first steps in achieving the Messianic era and ultimate redemption. Kalischer's lifelong efforts to raise funds to develop Eretz Israel, to deflect plans for the settlement of refugees in other lands, to persuade Jews to work the land in Palestine, and (sometimes overlooked by his supporters) to ensure competence on the part of new immigrants vividly illustrate the enormity of the task. The following account illustrates each of these problems and how Kalischer tried (not always successfully), to solve them.

Prominent amongst those who warned against the dangers of settling Eretz Israel was Rabbi Joseph Schwartz of Bavaria. In 1863 Schwartz wrote an open letter to Rabbi Eliyahu Gutmacher, published in the *Ha-magid* newspaper, saying that work for settlement could succeed only on three conditions. First, he said, tens of thousands of men must be made available to guard the land and workers against robbers and murderers. Second, necessary capital sums for development should be available, and thirdly, there must be immigrants who had known from their youth how to work the land, since the inhabitants themselves had neither the skill nor the desire to work in agriculture.

Although Schwartz's challenge was a serious critique of Kalischer's proposals, the latter remained unimpressed. He replied in *Ha-magid* that the prophet Nehemiah returned to Eretz Israel from Babylon in the year

---

[15] *Op. cit.,* 240.

537 C.E. with only forty-two thousand people and many enemies, but they nevertheless prevailed, half of them with arms and the other half employed in building the country. With respect to money, he pointed out that land in the country was cheap. Fifty thousand talents could buy many fields and vineyards and there were rich Jews, any one of whom could have bought all the fields and vineyards in the country.

Finally, Kalischer referred to three hundred letters that Sir Moses Montefiore's secretary had received from potential immigrants, half of which showed that the writers were trained in agriculture and prepared to work in it, and the other half from people learning Torah who had the strength to work in fields and vineyards.[16]

Jews in Agriculture: The Quality of the Soil

Apart from the views expressed by Rabbi Schwartz, there was a widespread belief that two thousand years of exile, during which few Jews took part in agricultural activities, resulted in a dearth of Jews who knew how to work the land. Although this argument had some substance (the facts were not in dispute), nevertheless there was proof that despite the problems and dissociation of Jews from agriculture, many enthusiastic groups were prepared to work the land. "One of the inhabitants of Jerusalem, a zaddik (righteous person) who has lived in Jerusalem for about thirty years, has obtained more than one hundred signatures of Ashkenazim who want to work on the land, and there are about one thousand Sephardim as well."[17]

In another letter written in 1869, he referred to many Jews in Russia who worked the land there and "wait only to begin the process of settling Eretz Israel so that they can immigrate with their possessions and carry out the mitzvot of terumot [free-will offerings, or tithes] and working the Holy Land."[18]

Kalischer was also aware of the doubts that had been expressed as to the quality of the land itself, and to be sure of the facts he sent his son to investigate. He reported that the land was fertile, and in Jerusalem some

---

[16] *Op. cit.*, 49–50.
[17] *Op. cit.*, 217.
[18] *Op. cit.*, 299.

three hundred men had already registered for this kind of work. The report also added several proposals for turning those who lived on charity into field workers; unfortunately, the resistance to productive work that had built up over the centuries proved too strong to overcome and nothing came of them. In addition, those who depended on charitable donations opposed efforts to raise money for agricultural settlement out of fear that as a result the financial support they had received would be substantially reduced. Still, Kalischer refused to conclude that his proposals were impracticable.

Apart from Rabbi Schwartz, other influential voices warned of difficulties. For example, in 1864 the editor of the *London Jewish Chronicle* criticized the Berlin Society for the Settlement for Jews in Eretz Israel for having failed to ascertain whether their aims were acceptable to the Jews already living in Eretz Israel or that there was satisfactory provision for the lives and property of settlers outside the cities. The paper maintained that in the opinion of the Turkish authorities, Jewish farmers would not be safe.

Kalischer replied that the article was based on outdated information. He wrote that the Turkish authorities punished severely any Arabs who committed acts of violence and took steps to prevent such acts. He further pointed out that in a letter to a Jewish merchant, Consul Rosin had stated it was easy to provide security there. In a characteristic flourish, Kalischer remarked that opposition to an idea is not deterred even by the "Holy of Holies" and criticized the *Jewish Chronicle* for being "so taken with material matters that they could not see the spiritual benefits."

Other influential voices either warned of difficulties in Eretz Israel or suggested that Jews emigrate to other countries. For example, Yehudah Horowitz, a journalist who supported a proposal to settle the Jews of Romania in the United States, wrote that the land in Eretz Israel was poor and provided no opportunities for merchants or craftsmen (most Romanian Jews fell into one of these categories), while America was a developed, wealthy country.

In his reply, Kalischer tried to compare the situation in Eretz Israel favorably to that in America – "Israel had capitalists, merchants, artists and shopkeepers. Only those who had no spirit could contemplate immigration elsewhere."[19]

Another serious and detailed critique of Kalischer's proposals was written by an anonymous correspondent calling himself Ish Meushar (Happy Man), who enumerated the difficulties of settling Turkish Jews in Eretz Israel. He said that having spoken to consuls and other experts, he had reached the conclusion that the time for immigration was simply not ripe. The reasons for this position were:

1. there was no living to be made from agriculture
2. it was difficult to buy land legally
3. Jews could live only in the cities because Moslems and Christians already lived in the villages
4. the climate was difficult and the police were corrupt.

He added that immigration could only take place with the support of a European power so long as the Turkish government was weak, and he pointed out that large sums of capital were required. Finally, settlements must have a military base as a defense against attack.[20]

Kalischer replied in kind, outlining answers to each charge. The Turkish police protected villagers, he said, and he said there were letters from Safed, Tiberias and Jaffa with signed by several hundred people stating the land was fertile and that they wanted to work. He cited two distinguished Jews living in Eretz Israel, Rabbi David Bashi and Karl Netter, each of whom stated that there was no fear on the part of the population, nor were there serious obstacles to working the land.

Sabbath Observance

Rabbi Azriel Hildesheimer, one of Kalischer's most influential supporters, was troubled by the possibility that there would be widespread non-observance of the traditional halachot that regulate the Sabbath. Kalischer assured him that the new Yishuv would "appoint guards and police as did Nehemiah so that there would not be

---

[19] *Op. cit.*, 442–443.
[20] *Op. cit.*, 262.

profanation of the Sabbath by the workers, all of whom will have to stay in nearby towns from the beginning to the end of the Sabbath in order to pray and learn there."[21] Reports of Shabbat violations continued and years later Kalischer again wrote to Hildesheimer, wondering: "How we can suspect the children of Israel in the Holy Land of being like those in Europe who… profane the Sabbath openly?"[22]

There does not appear to be any further reference to alleged breaches of the Sabbath in Kalischer's writings or reports, but the problem remained and troubled Rabbi Samuel Mohliver some years later.

Contact with and Support of Societies for Settlement in Eretz Israel

In addition to the letters and articles mentioned above, Kalischer maintained constant correspondence with societies in Europe whose purpose was to encourage settlement by raising funds and sending them to Eretz Israel. He defended his views as set out in *Derishat Zion* and refuted adverse reports about the prospects of establishing settlements. For example, he became involved with the Society for the Settlement of Israel, founded in 1860 by Dr. Chaim Luria and centered in Frankfurt-am-Main, to which he donated the proceeds of *Derishat Zion*. Luria believed that the 1848 revolutions that rocked Europe signified the beginnings of a process that would eventually lead to the Messianic era and the redemption of the Jewish people, but only if they returned to Eretz Israel, where their souls would awaken and where they would be cleansed of the impurity they had accumulated during the years of exile.

The Society was supported by many eminent Jewish leaders in Europe, with the notable exception of Moses Montefiore. Kalischer's task was to raise money, attract members and undertake propaganda on behalf of the society. He also took part in its Conference in 1863.

Unfortunately, a series of internal disputes reduced the Society's effectiveness and eventually led to its demise. In 1865, Kalischer and his friend Gutmacher founded a new society to carry on the work of their earlier days, and from then on, all matters regarding settlement in Eretz Israel appear to have been in Kalischer's hands.

---

[21] *Op. cit.,* 198–199.
[22] *Op. cit.,* 255.

Fundraising

Reference has been made to Kalischer's fund-raising in the financial and communal world. It is worth describing at length his letter to Asher Anschel Rothschild, who represented the Rothschild banking family in Frankfurt-am-Main. Kalischer preceded what he hoped would result in a personal interview with a long letter setting out his ideas and the practical steps he envisaged for returning the Jewish people to its land. The letter reflects many of Kalischer's strengths and weaknesses in achieving the goals he had set himself. In his introduction to the main theme of the letter, he heaps praise on Rothschild:

> The hair on my head stood up from fear. The pangs as of one giving birth seized me. How should a mosquito like myself enter through the gate of the king whose name is great amongst the nations and all the kings of the earth bow down before him? A man for whom the nobility seek his gold and he grants their request? Why has God done all this to one man? [...] This is only because from the redeemer of Jesse he will flower [a reference to the descendants of King David – RG].

> The real wonder is that the man who has all this is God-fearing, and even more wonderful it is that he judges through God and not by the sight of his eyes, [saying:] How great is my wealth.... He seeks only the Holy One, Blessed be He, to do justly and righteously and be with the modest of the earth.... He considers all his money and wealth as nothing compared to the love of God and doing charity and walking humbly with the creator of the Universe.

Kalischer then quotes at length from the Prophets, who promise a return of the Jewish people to their land, the construction of the Temple and reinstitution of the sacrificial service. For Kalischer this is clearly the primary purpose of resettling the land.

At the end of the letter, Kalischer asks, "Who knows whether it was just for this purpose that God gave him [Rothschild] great wealth and riches?" He added that if he could not persuade the Pasha, the ruler of the area in which Palestine was included, perhaps Rothschild could buy Jerusalem or at least the site of the Temple Mount, and Polish Jews could settle and worship there. At the end of the letter he made the extraordinary suggestion that Rothschild might buy another country and give it to the Sultan in exchange for Palestine.

This letter showed a complete failure to understand the likely reaction of an eminent banker who could not be expected to read long Biblical passages, particularly those about the reinstitution of the sacrifices, quoted to support a simple request for money that would enable Jews to settle in Israel. According to Kalischer, such settlement would be the first step towards the redemption of the Jewish people and the establishment of a Jewish state (a term that he specifically used). Not surprisingly, he received no reply.

Kalischer met with somewhat better success with Sir Moses Montefiore. As the result of Kalischer's influence, Montefiore attempted to obtain fifty-year land leases in many villages in which settlers could live. Unfortunately, the project did not materialize, though Montefiore managed to purchase one parcel of land in Jaffa in 1856.

Kalischer was punctilious in ensuring that funds raised were sent to the institution and for the purposes they were given. In 1870 he wrote to a certain Rabbi Mizrachi to express his distress that funds raised for settlements were diverted to the poor, stressing that money given for one purpose must never be used for another.[23]

Kalischer traveled widely in Germany and other parts of Europe in order to raise money for the Society for the Settlement of Eretz Israel. He enlisted the support of Rabbi Nathan Friedland, with whom he maintained a constant and active connection. Friedland had expressed ideas similar to those of Kalischer, including the idea that "redemption would come little by little" through settlement in Eretz Israel, and he also traveled widely to propagate this idea.

Friedland gladly agreed to raise funds for the Society and, in 1865, met with Adolph Cremieux, the President of the Alliance Israélite Universelle, and persuaded him to work on behalf of the settlements in

---

[23] *Op. cit.,* 310–313.

Eretz Israel. As a result of this meeting, the Alliance included support of the settlements in its sphere of activity. Nevertheless, the Alliance did not become a major contributor to the funds that Kalischer raised, no doubt because its constitution provided for worldwide activities but did not mention Eretz Israel.

Kalischer followed conditions in Eretz Israel closely, particularly opportunities for the purchase of land. When the Turkish authorities eased restrictions on buying land, Kalischer tried to take advantage of the situation as much as the money he had collected would allow. He wrote, "Now that we have merited receiving permission from the government to buy land in the Holy Land, it is as though God has called out to us, 'Come, buy it and carry out the commandments that depend on the land.'"

At the same time, Kalischer received reports that security in the settlements had improved, which increased his desire to move forward with his plans to buy land. He wished to make sure that representatives in Eretz Israel would not experience delays in receiving funds and using them for suitable projects. He approached a certain Rabbi Giron, an emigrant from Turkey in 1872, who agreed to carry out these tasks. In 1873, he negotiated purchases of land near Jericho, the tomb of Shimon ha-Zaddik in Jerusalem and in and around Jaffa.

Although Kalischer's difficulties increased with the death of Rabbi Giron, he was fortunate to find a worthy successor in Rabbi Abraham Ashkenazi, the Rishon le-Zion, who, together with a businessman from Jerusalem and Jaffa, managed to buy land in the village of Motza, near Jerusalem, in the summer of the following year. This was the first purchase of land with funds collected by his society.

Kalischer, who was entirely practical in his approach to fundraising, was not easily persuaded to support proposals that he considered impractical or potentially counterproductive. For example, he balked at a suggestion that German Chancellor Otto Bismarck be asked to pressure the Sultan of Turkey to ease restrictions on the purchase of land in Eretz Israel. Kalischer advised against the proposal because he feared that Bismarck would consult advisors who opposed the settlement project and whose report would therefore be negative. If that were to happen, it might become even more difficult to buy land. He suggested a direct request to the Sultan to make land available for the specific purpose of settling Jews from Persia, Romania and Russia.[24] Like Alkalai, Kalischer also encouraged Diaspora Jewry to support the Yishuv financially.

In typical fashion, Kalischer approached the Society for Settlement in Eretz Israel with an urgent request for money and specific details of his needs, including a report showing how much had already been donated and the steps required for settling land that was already available for purchase. He urged immediate action for fear that another prospective purchaser might step in.[25]

At the same time, he replied to Jews from Romania who needed assistance in their immigration with a series of practical questions, including their number, whether there was enough money to buy agricultural tools and livestock, who their leaders were and what communications facilities they possessed.[26]

Kalischer was known not only for his integrity, but also for striking a fair balance between competing claims for financial assistance. For example, when he was asked to advise the trustees of a fund established by the will of an Italian Jew, one bequest to assist Jews in Jerusalem, Hebron, Safed and Tiberias failed to state whether the money should be given to Ashkenazim. Kalischer suggested it should be allocated in the same proportion as was customary in such a case – namely, two-thirds to Sephardim and one-third to Ashkenazim. He also suggested that part of the funds be used for settlements whose inhabitants were involved in both Torah learning and manual work (*Torah va-avodah,* a phrase that years later became the name and motto of Ha-Poel ha-Mizrachi, the religious workers' party – R.G.).

Rabbi Yitzhak Elchanan Spector (1817–1896), one of the most influential Ashkenazic rabbis of the nineteenth century, supported Kalischer's ideas and practical proposals and promised to persuade landlords and tenants to contribute one percent of the rents they received

---

[24] *Op. cit.,* 392.
[25] *Op. cit.,* 44.
[26] *Op. cit.,* 480–481.

to the costs of settlement in Eretz Israel, foreshadowing the institution of the shekel as a symbol of identification with the Zionist movement in later years. Spector also persuaded Abraham Lenkes, an outstanding speaker and publicist, to spread Kalischer's ideas throughout Germany, immediately adding four hundred activists to support the cause of settlement of Eretz Israel.

The Alliance Israélite Universelle

As stated above, Alliance President Adolph Cremieux was impressed by the proposals of Kalischer and Alkalai, but little help was forthcoming. At a meeting of the Alliance in 1866, Kalischer proposed that Eretz Israel join the Alliance and offered the Alliance twelve thousand francs to help to realize his society's aims. The proposal was unrealistic, both due to the small sum involved and the wide-ranging sphere of the Alliance's activities.

Nevertheless, as a result of his suggestion the Alliance eventually directed some of its energies to settlements in Eretz Israel and in 1869 founded an agricultural school there. Although Kalischer seemed to view the project with some enthusiasm, his contemporary, Alkalai, condemned it as insignificant and disapproved of the small scale of the Alliance's activities. However, Kalischer maintained a close connection with the Alliance and was able to persuade Cremieux to try to arrange for Russian Jews to immigrate to the country in order to escape persistent and wide-spread persecution in their country.

On the outbreak of the Franco-Prussian War in 1870 the Alliance ceased its activities in Israel and the Society for the settlement of Eretz Israel disbanded. Undeterred, Kalischer set up branches in Berlin and Frankfurt-am-Main, and continued his travels throughout Germany in order to raise money.

Personal Aliyah

Kalischer was sensitive to criticism that he never settled in Eretz Israel. He was invited to be the rabbi in Mikveh Israel, a suggestion that he received warmly, although he was concerned that his health might be affected by the climate. He asked two friends, Rabbi Gutmacher and

Abraham Landau, for their advice and blessing for such a move. Gutmacher advised Kalischer to accept the appointment but Landau advised him not to settle in Israel since he was needed in Europe. Kalischer remained in Europe but suffered pangs of conscience for doing so:

> The basis of my thought is to fulfill the mitzvah of living in Eretz Israel, which is a positive commandment…. Everyone ought to fulfill the mitzvah, but if they cannot, they should send their emissary, money, assistance or work. I hope that they [his critics] will believe me that after forty-four years my spirit throbs with the feeling of holiness and I have not slept from carrying out this work, from which I have received no remuneration. I have spent most of my money, although no one will believe me… because all the money that is brought in will be only for holy purposes. If I have no knowledge of agriculture, I will find men on whom I will set my sights to carry out the mitzvot diligently and then my opponents will also thank me.

Kalischer and the Reform Movement

In 1868 Kalischer criticized Reform Judaism for its opposition to resettlement of Eretz Israel, and especially over the movement's denial of the redemptive power of returning to the land in order to bring about the Davidic Messiah's arrival. To Reform Jews who believed that Judaism must change with the times, he replied that the Torah is "an everlasting statute for our generations" and therefore exists outside time. He wrote:

> If even one Christian or Muslim clergyman were to deviate from his religion, he would be immediately removed from his post. How can they (the Reformers) say 'I am a rabbi and I will be a shepherd' if they deny all the prophecies which are full of the visions of future redemption?… Not only do we wait for ourselves but we wait for all his creatures… all the inhabitants of the earth will exult and a light from above over His world when He redeems us.

Kalischer argued that the Jewish notion of the Chosen People differs from other versions of similar ideas. "Heaven and earth do not belong only to us," he wrote. "We are a people of truth who say that the righteous of all faiths have a share in the World to Come, and all faiths will recognize that we are the mother of all faiths because we accepted the Torah at Sinai; otherwise all nations would have remained idol-worshippers."

This letter was a clever critique of Reform Judaism because apart from the assertion that they were denying the absolute authority of the Torah, they were denying the settlement of Eretz Israel as the first step towards redemption not only of the Jewish people but through them of the whole world, which of course is the message of the Prophets. By stressing this universal aspect and purpose of traditional Judaism and return, Kalischer was able to use the Reform Movement's own language against it. Reform stressed the universality of the Jewish message that the Jews must spread among the nations. Kalischer pointed out that this was exactly Judaism's ultimate aim.[27]

Kalischer was staunchly opposed to compromise with the Reform Movement. In a letter to *Ha-magid* in 1869, he rejected a suggestion by Rabbi Joel of Breslau that Reform and Orthodox Jews could still pray together even though the Reform Movement omitted sections of the prayer service that included prayers for the restoration of sacrifices and future redemption. Kalischer quoted a passage from Maimonides that it was a mitzvah to hate those who deny Judaism's basic principles.[28] A similar suggestion, published in *Ha-ivri* in 1872 with the aim of avoiding a breach between the Reform and Orthodox, met with the same rebuff.[29]

Kalischer was in sharp conflict with Abraham Geiger, a Reform rabbi who preached that the mitzvot no longer apply in modern times and that the eternal hope of returning to the Land of Israel and rebuilding of the Temple must be abandoned. "The land where we live is our Jerusalem, and Europe is the Jerusalem of all humankind," he wrote. Kalischer's

---

[27] Klausner, *The Writings of Z.H. Kalischer*, 264–265.
[28] *Op. cit.,* 285–288, and Federbush, 53–55.
[29] *Op. cit.,* 363–364, and Federbush, 335–357.

reply was brief and devastating: if the mitzvot no longer applied, then they could not possibly be the word of God.

In the same letter he returned to his main preoccupation, calling upon all groups to join with the Society for the Settlement of Eretz Israel to support resettlement of the land and "the cultivation of holy produce in our land."[30]

Kalischer had justifiable fears about the reformers' seductive approach, and worried that in the era of the Emancipation, Reform would attract large segments of the Jewish community.

On the other hand, Kalischer seems to have had greater tolerance of secular Jews than for the Reform Movement. In a letter written in 1872, he expressed support for non-religious Jews who wished to work the land, pointing out that this in itself (as stressed in a later age by Rabbi A.I. Kook) was a great mitzvah. In a brief article in *Ivri anochi,* Kalischer specially praised the Society for the Settlement of Eretz Israel for encouraging settlements whose members he delicately described as "not of those who dwell in the tent of the Torah." In practice, he seems to have regarded the settlement of Eretz Israel as equivalent to all the other mitzvot.[31]

Summary

Kalischer was an unusual combination of idealist religious thinker and practical man of affairs. He possessed an integrity that would not allow any compromise in financial or religious issues. Whatever the temptation, he would not allow his Society for the Settlement of Eretz Israel to enter into a financial commitment unless the funds were available, and he was ruthless in criticizing any misapplication of funds, however pure the motive. He was usually a realist who did not allow his zeal for settlement in Eretz Israel to blind him to the difficulties that had to be overcome in developing the country, while on the other hand he corrected reports of conditions he considered to be accessibly negative.

---

[30] *Op. cit.,* 298–300.
[31] *Op. cit.,* 345.

Above all, despite severe criticism by the majority of outspoken rabbis in Eastern Europe, Drishat Zion was to become one of the main seeds from which grew religious Zionism.

Rabbi Samuel Mohliver   הרב שמואל מוהליבר

RABBI SAMUEL MOHLIVER
(1824–1898)

RABBI SAMUEL MOHLIVER was descended from twenty-two generations of great rabbinical figures. His mother's family were Hasidim and his paternal grandfather, Rabbi Joseph Morotok, was a student of Rabbi Chaim of Volozhin before the latter founded his yeshivah. Mohliver's father was also a great scholar in Talmud which he combined with secular education, excelling particularly in the field of accounting. He earned his living in trade but refused requests to serve as a rabbi until he assumed the rabbinate of Shalak in old age.

Like many outstanding rabbinic personalities, Mohliver was a child prodigy. At the age of four he was already thoroughly familiar with the Torah and many commentaries, large passages of which he could recite by heart. At the age of eight he began to study Talmud with his father, and only two years later was spoken of as a genius. His father ensured that his range of knowledge would not be confined to the Bible, the Talmud and their commentaries, and under the older man's guidance Mohliver became familiar with works of Jewish thought such as Yehudah Halevi's *Kuzari*, Maimonides's *Guide for the Perplexed* and Rabbenu Bachya's *Duties of the Heart*. He also studied Kabbalah and Hasidic thought and acquired wide knowledge of Jewish history, accountancy, engineering and astronomy.

Over the years he also learned Russian, German and Polish. His range of knowledge and interests indicated an approach to intellectual life similar to (although not so expressed) that of Samson Raphael Hirsch.

Marriage and Early Years in the Rabbinate

Married at the age of fifteen, Mohliver spent the next three years living with his in-laws in Haloboka, as was traditional at that time. He taught Talmud to the rabbis of the city and eventually was sent to study in the Volozhin Yeshiva, where he was granted rabbinic ordination. He did not wish to derive monetary benefit from his Torah learning and instead became a flax trader, devoting his spare time to learning and exchanging letters with the Gaon on questions of Halacha.

In 1848 Mohliver's in-laws died of the plague and his business began to collapse. As a result Mohliver regretfully accepted the position of Rabbi in Haloboka. Six years later he became the rabbi and head of the Beth Din of the city of Shaki where he remained for six years until he was appointed Rabbi of Suwalk, the provincial capital, a position which gave him an opportunity to extend his activities beyond the world of Torah learning and enter the wider community as a communal leader.

Soon afterwards, he had the opportunity to exercise his leadership talents. In 1863, thousands of Poles rebelled against Russian domination and the Czar's brutal rule. Many Jews suffered for having assisted the rebels, and Mohliver successfully petitioned the authorities to commute the death sentences of some Jews and to release others. More significantly, his public statements and addresses led to a general relaxation of the tension, and the local government eventually recognized his efforts by awarding him a medal.

Rabbinate in Radom

In 1868, Mohliver became the rabbi of Radom and the head of its rabbinical court. This position gave him opportunities for wider involvement in the community and his lectures attracted audiences from all around the area. His stature was such that he successfully maintained friendly relations with all groups in the city, including the Hasidic majority, even though he opposed their approach to Judaism on ideological grounds.

Fearing that he might be regarded as a rebbe or a *kadosh* (holy one) – common descriptions of Hassidic leaders – Mohliver took pains to

belong to them, and that one who denies that relationship actually denies the existence of God.

Zionism and Assimilation

Persecution had benefitted the Jewish people in that it gave rise to the Zionist movement. An unpersecuted minority living under foreign rule will generally adapt to the laws and customs of the country where they live, and in time they will assimilate. Since the Jews only became a nation by accepting the Torah, when the Torah is rejected nationhood is also rejected. The connection of the Jewish people to its land is a critical element in preserving its survival, said Reines, but on the other hand, the persecution of the Jewish People in the Diaspora is a clear sign that God wishes to ensure its continued existence.

Interestingly, Reines devoted a section of the book to a discussion of dress. He regarded attempts by many Jews to adopt styles of dress worn by local non-Jews as an attempt to blend in, and said that this only increased the hatred of the Jews.

Justifying the World Zionist Organization, Reines drew a far-fetched analogy with Hillel, whom a non-Jew once asked to teach him the Torah while he stood on one foot. The great sage accepted the challenge, telling the potential convert, "What is hateful to you, do not do to another. All the rest is commentary" (Tractate *Shabbat* 31a). Reines deduced from this story that there is great importance in bringing Jews who had strayed far from their people into the community if at all possible, and he stressed that one should maintain hope that such individuals would eventually return to Judaism. In his view, the World Zionist Organization had brought back many such Jews to identification with their people, and this was the very first step to Judaism.

Reines and the Opponents of Zionism

Reines distinguished between uniting with others as a means of achieving a common, specific purpose from joining them in order to follow in their footsteps. There could be no objection to joining others, even non-believers, in taking steps to save the Jewish people. Religious Jews worked with secularists all over the world on charitable projects when there was no danger of damaging religious observance, and the fact that secularists headed nearly all these institutions did not preclude cooperation. Similarly, there could be no objection to joining the World Zionist Organization.

Reines made an interesting observation about the fact that the leaders of the Zionist Organization were not religious. He considered it inevitable that a Jewish nationalist movement should be led by secularists because they were originally assimilationists who had learned that assimilation could not solve the problems of Jews in the Diaspora. This led to an awakening for secularists, eventually bringing them back to the concept of a Jewish nation. Since very few Orthodox Jews had ever subscribed to the dogma of assimilation, it was natural that the leaders of Jewish nationalism would be secular.

Reines was not satisfied merely with refuting attacks against the Zionists. He asserted that the Zionist movement was beneficial to religion for two reasons. First, Zionism was essentially a religious movement dedicated to performing a mitzvah based in the Torah, the mitzvah to settle the land. Second, the results that are likely to flow from the foundations of Zionism are consistent with the Torah and may increase religious observance.

He then made a subtle distinction between ends and means. While a means used to achieve a purpose may be material, it can lead to spiritual ends. For example, one must sharpen a knife in order to perform a circumcision, as one must cut wood in order to build a succah. So, too, with regard to Zionism: The World Zionist Organization is a material concern, but the goal – settlement of Eretz Israel – is spiritual.

The Religious and the Secular

Reines did not believe that the world can be divided neatly into categories of "righteous" and "wicked." He said that many levels lie between the two extremes and a majority exist somewhere in the middle. While the Zionist movement contained many anti-religious personalities and philosophies, Reines pointed out that not all Orthodox rabbis opposed Zionism: more than one hundred and fifty rabbis had declared their support for it, although many were afraid to state their opinions publicly for fear of being attacked by opponents.

He also pointed out that the differences between the secular and the religious surfaced only regarding matters where faith was involved – in other words, in ritual matters between human beings and God, but not in relationships between human beings. Therefore, why complain that the non-religious supported the idea of the return to Zion?

Near the end of the work, Reines makes interesting observations on the concept of peoplehood. In his view race, language, religion and a particular land are what make a people; of these elements, the land has the special role of protecting the others. In the same way that an individual cannot love another as much as he loves himself, so, too, one people cannot treat another people in the same way it treats itself, but a people scattered amongst the nations and living far from its national land cannot achieve the same rights as the indigenous population. To Reines, Eretz Israel is a refuge for the Jewish people.

Reines also attempted to deflect the charge by elements in the religious community that Zionism had to be opposed because it attempted to hasten the coming of the Messiah, which the majority of Orthodox rabbis believed had to come solely through divine intervention. Nevertheless, Reines wrote that the Zionist movement claimed to solve only the Jewish people's material problems, not their spiritual ones.

Reines rejected the idea that redemption would come by natural means. Rather, the Messiah would come when three conditions were met: when the Kingdom of Heaven had arrived, the Kingdom of David had been re-established, and the Holy Temple was built in Jerusalem. Settlement in Eretz Israel, he said, was the sign of the Jewish people's love for its land, which *it is hoped* will lead to redemption [emphasis added].

Diaspora and Redemption

For Reines, persecution was God's way of ensuring the continuation of the Jewish people in exile. When there is no persecution, he said, Jews assimilate. He believed that exile is both punishment for the sins of the Jewish people and a means of ensuring their survival and ultimate redemption. In the latter sense, it is a universal phenomenon, to be followed by the corollary that the Diaspora Jew should spread the ideas of the Torah to the nations of the world, who would then understand the benefits they receive from the Jewish people and the value of the Jewish religion. As a result, the nations would assist in the return to Eretz Israel, which would lead to redemption of both the Jewish people and the non-Jewish nations.

The spread of the Torah at the time of redemption would led to the rule of the intellect and the absence of rule of force; only when this occurred could the final redemption take place, and this would come by divine action. Unlike Alkalai and Kalischer, he makes no distinction between the Messiah of the House of Joseph and the Messiah of the House of David.

The Fourth Zionist Congress – 1900: The Dispute over "Culture"

Reines hesitated as to whether to join the official Zionist Movement and did not attend the Zionist Congress until its fourth meeting, where he was immediately confronted with a fundamental dispute concerning education. The secular leadership of the World Zionist Organization intendedto include in its activities such cultural subjects as Jewish history, Bible, geographic knowledge of Eretz Israel, Hebrew and the intellectual foundations of Zionism. Reines joined with other religious delegates in opposing the proposal, fearing, with justification, that non-religious and, in some cases, anti-religious attitudes would permeate the teaching.

Speaking in Hebrew (apparently unusual in early Congresses, and it is doubtful whether all, or even a majority, of delegates understood the language), Reines pleaded that the Congress not enter the field of culture on which there were so many conflicting views about both content and approach. Nachum Sokolow and Max Nordau were effusive in their praise of Reines's speech, but the attempt to reject the proposed cultural committee ultimately failed.[8]

A small committee comprised of Ahad ha'Am, Reines and Sokolow was appointed to consider the problem with the president and make

---

[8] Bat-Yehudah, Geulah. *Ish ha-Meorot*, 109.

recommendations to the Conference. The committee proposed on Achad ha'Am's suggestion that since there were two streams in the Organization – the traditional/national and the progressive/national – there should be two committees independent of each other to reflect their respective views. This proposal was accepted by the Conference.[9]

Reines remained uneasy about what had been achieved (and not achieved) at the Russian Conference. In a circular to Mizrachi groups, he pointed defensively to the rapid growth of Mizrachi, which had grown to include 130 branches in just six months. The Organization managed to block Ahad ha'Am's proposal to establish one committee for cultural matters, while Reines attacked mainstream Orthodox Jews who had not joined the Mizrachi and could have helped in opposing the secular leaders of the Zionist movement. He pointed to Mizrachi's success in limiting the Jewish National Fund to buying land in Eretz Israel, but it is clear that Reines was not happy that he had failed to get "culture" removed entirely from the Zionist agenda. He remained uneasy at the establishment of a non-religious cultural stream; but he no doubt felt that the result of the debates was the best that could have been achieved, and he was probably right. Had his proposed compromise proposal failed to gain acceptance, there would have been only one, secular stream of education in the Zionist Organization, which probably would have made it impossible for Reines to keep a majority of Mizrachi supporters in the Organization.

Religious Zionists and Orthodox Rabbis

The majority of the rabbis, and as a consequence, many religious Jews in Europe, were opposed in the first place to the Chovevei Zion and subsequently to the Zionist movement. Efforts by Reines and others associated with the movement to persuade skeptics that there was nothing objectionable in Zionism's aims met with little success. One example was a meeting held with the Gerer Rebbe, whom, even after forceful and persuasive arguments, Reines could not move. (Sefer Plonsk and its Environs – Tel-Aviv). Even a written opinion by him and other

---

[9] *Op. cit.,* 158–160.

rabbis that there was nothing objectionable in the aims of the Zionist movement did not improve the position.

Fifth Zionist Congresses – 1902: the Founding of Mizrachi

At the Fifth Zionist Congress, the debate concerning culture continued. Reines spoke and debated with Sokolow, Chaim Weizmann and others, repeating the arguments that he had used at the previous Congresses. The resolution proposing cultural activities was nevertheless passed, and Orthodox members were left with two alternatives – either to leave the Zionist movement or to remain and continue the struggle from within.

Reines chose the second course and organized the religious members of the organization into a bloc, as the proponents of culture had already done; this new bloc formed the nucleus of a new group, eventually called Mizrachi of which Reines became the leader. Those who left the Zionist Movement formed what became known as Agudat Israel.

At the same time, however, Reines was under intense pressure to sever his connection with the Zionist movement altogether. Rabbi Yisrael Meir Kagan, who was known as the Chofetz Chaim and the leader of the traditional Eastern European rabbis, traveled for three hours in order to persuade Reines to break with the secularists. Although the Chofetz Chayim warned him that a refusal to leave the movement would result in isolation from mainstream Orthodoxy, Reines refused to budge. As a result, he was excluded from gatherings of the rabbinical establishment.

The episode provides an illustration of Reines's stature among Orthodox authorities: He was regarded as a great halachic authority and destined to be a pivotal figure in the rabbinical world. He wore his expulsion from mainstream Orthodoxy as a mark of rabbinical eminence, and the unbridled denigration to which he had been accustomed was intensified.

First Mizrachi Conference – 1902

The Mizrachi organization's first conference was held in Vilna in 1902. Some sixty delegates attended. Reines was elected chairman of the new organization, and leading rabbis agreed with Reines that the task of

Zionism was to save persecuted Jews and those who were in danger of assimilation, with no connection to religious redemption.

However, differences of opinion about culture continued, as they had at the Zionist Congress. Rabbi Yitzhak Nissenbam argued that without learning Jewish history, the Hebrew language and geography of Eretz Israel, Zionism would be empty of content. However, the Conference decided, as Reines wished, that Mizrachi would forego cultural issues and concentrate only on political ones.

On the other hand, the Conference decided that individual branches of Mizrachi would be free to decide whether or not to be involved in cultural activities. When Reines pressed for the publication of literature to be recommended by the Organization and of original propaganda on its behalf, his views were accepted.

The Conference both illustrated Reines's approach to Zionist activities and stood in contrast to those views. Reines supported the decision to allow local Mizrachi groups to carry on cultural activities, a move that "political" Mizrachists strongly opposed. Those who opposed any kind of cultural activity saw Reines's support for localized cultural activities as a back-handed way of involving the organization in culture, and it may be assumed that when Reines realized the Conference would not accept his blanket opposition to any kind of cultural work, he decided that at least he could ensure central control of any publications issued by the organization.

Connections with Mizrachi Branches and Publicity

In addition to journeys all over Russia to provide support for existing Mizrachi groups and to form new ones, Reines corresponded regularly with all sections of the movement and spent time replying to many inquiries. In 1902, he published the periodical *From the Mizrachi,* whose primary purpose was to provide news about the movement and about the Zionist movement as a whole.

In the magazine's second issue, Reines said that it should deal only with political issues and should not touch subjects that could cause dissension in the ranks. In his contributions to the periodical he stressed the political aims of Zionism, saying immigration to Eretz Israel that led to a future Jewish state should unite believers and unbelievers. In one article, Reines made an uncharacteristically impractical suggestion that Jews should save money by eating the same kind of food on Shabbat as on week days, and the money saved should be devoted to the cause of the Mizrachi and Zionism.

It is relevant to mention that Reines, as indicated in the debates over accepting vacant lands in Uganda, was an admirer and friend of Herzl. In 1902, he sent a copy of *Or Chadash* with a note expressing admiration to Herzl for having sacrificed everything in order to found and develop the Zionist Movement. His use of the term "sacrifice" was prophetic; Herzl's early death just two years later may well have been at least partly caused by his exertion in founding and leading the Zionist movement.

Ha-Mizrachi

Reines felt that the time had now come to formalize the Mizrachi Organization with declared aims and a constitution as well as a program that worked for the future, in particular in the field of public relations. It also had to prepare for the coming Sixth Zionist Congress which was scheduled to take place in Basel, Switzerland in August, 1903.

In that year, the organization published the first issue of *Ha-mizrachi,* a monthly magazine intended to be the movement's literary organ. In its first issue, Reines set out shortly his own answers to those who criticized the Zionist Movement. It did not anticipate or propose to anticipate the coming of the Messiah, he said; rather, the aim of Zionism was to save persecuted Jews who could not live anywhere outside Israel.

Regarding Mizrachi's affiliation to the secular Zionist movement, he said that religious-secular collaboration was nothing new, and pointed out that even very Orthodox groups routinely joined secularists and others for charitable work without protests of any kind. Oddly, he did not reply specifically to the criticism that the Zionist Organization had decided to enter the field of culture. He simply remarked that if more Orthodox Jews had joined the Zionist Movement, this question would not have arisen.

The Massacres in Kishinev in 1903

Following the anti-Jewish pogroms in Kishinev in April, 1903, Reines immediately wrote to Herzl asking whether he should try to persuade the Alliance Israélite Universelle to use their resources to bring destitute Jews to Eretz Israel and approach the Russian government to take steps to prevent further persecution. He also suggested that governments in London, Paris and Berlin should be approached to participate in relief work. Herzl rejected the proposals, as he had done to a similar request by Ussishkin, in the following terms:

> I understand the sorrow which the news of the disaster that was suffered by the Jews of Russia has caused you. However, I do not agree with the approach suggested by you. Similar conitions… in other countries and we have not found a cure for them.[10]

The Sixth Zionist Congress and the Uganda Plan

The Sixth Zionist Congress in 1903 was dominated by debate over the Uganda Plan. Herzl announced that the British government had offered Jewish groups an opportunity to colonize the central African region of Uganda, and he encouraged the Congress to accept the offer subject to a satisfactory report by a committee of enquiry. Herzl stressed the need to establish a temporary haven for Jews whose plight had to be relieved urgently and said that afterwards, they would be settled in Eretz Israel. The struggle for immigration to Eretz Israel and the achievement of statehood would continue.

Russian delegates to the Congress were particularly uncompromising in their opposition to the plan, to the extent that they considered demanding Herzl's resignation. They considered any proposal that involved a temporary substitute for Eretz Israel as treachery and proposed that Herzl's prerogatives as president be limited.

Reines demanded they retract their criticism and threatened to sever his connection with them should they fail to do so. He continued to support Herzl, saying, "With all our heart we believe in the sincerity of

---

[10] *Op. cit.,* 163–164. Also see Y. Raphael, "Reines's Letters to Herzl." *Sinai* 3, 339 and following.

his motives… which are all entirely for the good of our people and we will always assist him in the holy work he has undertaken."[11] He accused the Russians of being more concerned with land than with people who, he wrote "are more precious to us than the land." In effect, Reines was saying that ensuring the safety of Jews and the survival of the Jewish people took precedence over settling the Land of Israel and achieving a Jewish state. In order to attain these goals, he was willing to consider any and all proposals.

Herzl considered resigning over its issue but was dissuaded at least partly by Reines, who wrote to him in the following terms: "No, dear brother, Heaven forbid that you should say things like this! The people of Israel need you and your devoted work. And who are the few men… on whose account you would leave your people and land and cease this holy work?"[12]

Reines wrote a memorandum to Mizrachi delegates setting out clearly the arguments for and against the proposal. He called on group members to achieve a consensus and avoid "ruin and disaster… do not endanger Zionism."[13] Arguments in favor included:

1. The Uganda Plan did not negate the struggle for Eretz Israel
2. It would achieve an independent Jewish state
3. It would show the practicability of a Jewish settlement that would in due course support the implementation of the Zionist dream
4. The right of the Jewish people to Eretz Israel would remain in force (were this not so, the proposal would have been rejected out of hand)

Arguments against the plan were:

1. The proposal conflicted with the Basel program of the World Zionist Organization; namely, that the purpose of the organization was to settle Jews in Eretz Israel.

---

[11] *Sinai* 3; *Encyclopedia of Religious Zionism*, 671.
[12] *Sinai* 3; *Encyclopedia of Religious Zionism*, 670–671.
[13] *Ibid.*

2. It would mortally weaken the fight for Eretz Israel because the world would see Uganda as a substitute and the energies of the Jewish people would be diverted to the project.

3. Eretz Israel involved the return by Jews to their spiritual home, which is of basic importance to every Jew. Uganda could not claim any such connection which was proved by the failure of the project for Jewish settlement in Argentina.

Reines agonized over the issue and discussed his doubts, fears and feelings in a letter to Israel Zangwill (1864–1926), an Anglo-Jewish novelist who had founded the Jewish Territorial Organization to arrange for the emigration of Jews from countries in which they were persecuted to different areas around the world. After much debate, Reines addressed the Mizrachi Organization in tears, urging the group to vote for the proposal as it would provide immediate relief to destitute and persecuted Jews. He made it clear that he did not intend to cease the struggle for Eretz Israel as a permanent home for the Jewish people.

Internally, there was a fierce debate within Mizrachi on this question. Reines stated specifically that Uganda could become a material and spiritual home for the Jewish people. Influenced by Reines, the majority decided to vote in favor of the proposal, but in view of the strong, fundamental differences on the issue, Mizrachi did not vote as a party at the Congress.

Reines eventually abstained from the vote, a move that was interpreted as vacillation. His position in the Mizrachi organization was weakened as a result of his final vote in Congress supporting Herzl. He had broken with the delegates from Russia, all of whom voted against the Uganda plan. As a result, he was not elected to the Russian group's Executive Committee. Even a proposal by the Chairman of the Standing Committee to make Reines a deputy member of the Working Committee was rejected.

Since Reines's support of the Zionist Movement was based entirely on the need to save Jews from persecution and assimilation, his decision to vote for the Uganda project was logical and consistent with his approach to Zionism. He was not ideologically a Zionist. Probably as a result, Herzl and Reines, were invited together with others to meet the Interior Minister of Russia in December, 1903 in order to obtain permission to open a branch of the National Bank (the financial arm of the Zionist movement) in Russia.

Eventually Great Britain withdrew its offer, partly due to the strong opposition in Congress. Still, there were continuing reverberations of the dispute within the Zionist movement. Reines tried to find common ground between the various factions in relation to the Uganda matter and other issues, and he suggested a special meeting between representatives of the Russian delegates, Mizrachi and the Zionist leaders to achieve a compromise. This was not practical and Reines eventually accused the Russian delegates of obstructing the Congress by refusing to accept its decisions.

This post-Congress episode was out of character for Reines because he ignored the fact that only three groups were entitled to settle disputes of that kind – Congress itself, its full executive committee and the smaller executive committee. It is surprising that Reines did not understand the correct constitutional method of dealing with the matter.

The Mizrachi Conference in Pressburg, 1904

Following the battle over the Uganda Plan, Reines came under attack from all sides. He was criticized by members of the Mizrachi Party for supporting Herzl, he was under constant attack by the bulk of Orthodox rabbis who regarded his support of Zionism and his general willingness to compromise as heresy, and as Mizrachi prepared to hold its annual conference in Pressburg, Slovakia, local rabbis called on the town to boycott the conference and observe "the true, authentic faith given to us at Sinai." These attacks sapped the foundations of his authority.

Reines responded to Orthodox attacks in the Hebrew newspaper *Tel Talpiot,* saying that all the passages quoted by the rabbis against him could be interpreted as supporting Zionism and the Mizrachi Movement. Moreover, he said, many rabbis and Torah sages cited passages from traditional Jewish texts to support the ideas that motivated Hibbat Zion and Zionism. He called on his opponents to justify their opposition with facts and supporting texts and challenged them to quote the relevant sources in public. If they could not, he said, then their attacks were of no significance.

In the event, the delegates received a warm welcome in the city, and Reines' characteristic moderation helped defuse a heated debate about admitting as a member a person who was not observant. Reines, quoting the Talmudic sage Hillel, said the group should act according to Hillel's welcoming approach.

Decline

The first clear indication of Reines's decline came at Pressburg, when a resolution was passed in his absence to move the center of the party to Frankfurt-am-Main out of fear that the Russian government would hinder the group's operations following the Kishinev massacre in 1903, when the police failed to restrain rioters in order to save Jewish lives and property. When Reines returned, he objected strongly and a long dispute ensued on the possibility of rescinding the resolution.

Rabbi Nobel, a delegate from Germany, suggested that the central committee should be in Frankfurt, but said there should be a separate committee in Russia to operate there. The proposal was disingenuous: power would effectively lie in Germany, which was obviously the intention. From this point, Reines's influence in the organization gradually waned.

The Seventh Zionist Congress – 1905

As the Mizrachi prepared for the seventh Zionist Congress, Reines repeated his views about Eretz Israel, the Uganda plan and other items on the Congress agenda. Mizrachi, he wrote categorically, rejected the ideas of the territorialist movement, which he claimed was contrary to the Torah. No religious Jew could consider any country as a substitute for Eretz Israel, he said, but nevertheless repeated arguments for and against accepting other territories while stressing the necessity of practical work in Eretz Israel which "was the basis of our building a state in the future."

Mizrachi was criticized in *Die Welt,* the Zionist newspaper, for being concerned only with religion and the desire to force religious requirements on the delegates. Reines replied that those allegations were false and would only cause hatred of a large Zionist party. The issue was a poignant illustration of the future relationship between religious and non-religious groups in the State of Israel. The background to this criticism may well have been the comparative lack of religious settlements in the nineteenth and early twentieth centuries.

In a circular to the Mizrachi, Reines set out views concerning the Zionist Organization as compared to the Hibbat Zion movement. Zionism was a historic movement that arose out of the "process of Diaspora life" in all its forms and varieties, was based on the attitudes of the whole people, and took into account the interests of other nations. In contrast, the activities of Hibbat Zion had no order or system, "had no basis in the present and no hope for the future." Political Zionism could not by its very nature be compared to Hibbat Zion.

The Yeshiva at Lida

Despite his unsuccessful attempt to establish a yeshiva, Reines had never given up the idea of trying again. He ascribed the decline of Jewish communities in Western Europe to their ignorance of traditional Jewish sources and Jewish history, placing special emphasis on recruiting laymen in professions or in trade who were the backbone of religious life. He managed to garner support for the idea in the Mizrachi Party.

His dream was eventually realized at Lida. The subjects taught there were identical to those of the earlier yeshiva and included studies in Talmud, Hebrew language, Jewish history and secular subjects. The yeshiva attracted students from all over Europe. Although his support came largely from Mizrachists, Reines did not allow this to affect the subjects chosen or the ways in which they were taught.

Predictably, the yeshiva was attacked by Orthodox elements who had long opposed Reines, but they were unable to prevent its successful establishment and development. On average, some three hundred students studied there.

Some suggested the yeshiva ought to be in Israel. Accepting the criticism, Reines responded, "Eretz Israel is not yet a spiritual center that can shed the light of Torah in the lands of the Exile." Furthermore, the yeshiva was needed in Russia, where there was a large Jewish population and where assimilation was making inroads into the Jewish people. His comment reflected clearly the spiritual condition of the Jews in the Diaspora and Eretz Israel at the time.

The Tenth Zionist Congress, 1911

As before, the issue of culture was an important subject of discussion at the Congress, and the Congress decided once more that official Zionism would pursue cultural activities as well as political ones. Hebrew, Jewish history and about Eretz Israel would be taught, but nothing would be taught that conflicted with Judaism, although observance was left as a matter for the individual.

The cultural committee on which Reines sat made two proposals: that a small executive committee unify and organize cultural activities in Eretz Israel and the countries of the East, and that no institution of the Zionist Organization do anything that conflicted with the Jewish religion.

The failure to remove the matter of culture from the Congress's agenda resulted in a split in the Mizrachi Movement. Following this decision to support cultural programming, members of the organization vanguard met in order to plan a united reaction to this final rejection of their proposals. The center in Frankfurt suggested they should leave the Zionist Organization, whereas Reines threw the whole weight of his influence against the decision. His words are significant: "I choose to join with secular Zionists who desire the unity of the people rather than join with Orthodox Jews who wish to destroy it."

The large majority accepted Reines's views and decided to remain within the Organization, continuing the struggle to preserve religious norms within the Zionist movement. However, a minority withdrew from the Zionist Organization to form Agudat Israel.

Having been defeated on the matter of substance, Reines worked hard to obtain the maximum representation for Mizrachi on the relevant committees in order to influence the development of the new department. After negotiations, it was agreed that the Chairman of Mizrachi would join the World Zionist Organization Executive Committee as an adviser. A six-member cultural committee, of which three members would be from Mizrachi, would refer any problem of a religious nature to a rabbi acceptable to both sides.

Reines must have realized Mizrachi's weakness in this arrangement: decisions would remain solely in the hands of the executive committee, which could ignore the adviser's views. Nevertheless, in a letter to Mizrachi members that appeared in the *Ha-ivri* newspaper in 1912, Reines set out the arguments for remaining in the Zionist Organization and predicted (wrongly) that Mizrachi representation in the organization would grow, increasing the party's representation at Zionist Congresses. He predicted the Zionist movement would support Mizrachi educational institutions and argued that this could not be achieved if they seceded.

Reines and the German Rabbis

Although Reines tried to maintain peace with the newly-formed Agudat Israel, a furious attack by Agudah chairman Dr. Jacob Breuer at the first Agudah conference in 1912 strained relations between them.

Breuer was a German Jew, which added salt to Reines's wounds over the formation of the Agudah after having been annoyed over the move of the Mizrachi executive to Frankfurt. He refused to meet with a delegation of German rabbis.

Reines and Personal Aliya

Like Kalischer before him, Reines was sensitive to the possible accusation that he himself had never settled in Eretz Israel. He wrote to his friend, disciple and successor Rabbi Yehudah Maimon, "I wish to see with my own eyes the land on whose behalf I have devoted my strength, but when I go there I do not wish to be dependent on others." However, World War I broke out, and Reines never realized his dream.

Reines and the Hebrew University

Despite major efforts by Reines and his supporters, only thirty-eight representatives of Mizrachi, out of 540 total delegates, attended the eleventh Zionist Congress in Vienna in 1913. Although Reines was elected honorary president of Mizrachi before to the Congress, his influence continued to decline. When Chaim Weizmann and Menachem

Ussishkin proposed that a Hebrew University be established, Reines could do little more than express "confidence" that men and women would not study together. He had fallen sadly out of touch with the Zionist Organization, becoming badly disillusioned with the organization that he had believed would become so observant that there would be no need for a separate Mizrachi faction at all.

Although the Vienna meeting marked the rise of Rabbi Maimon within the Mizrachi Movement, the new leader's rise to prominence was anything but auspicious. The man who would play a vital role in religious Zionism for the next fifty years made two proposals to the Congress, both of which were rejected.

First, he asked that the religious school Tachkemoni be permitted to join the general network of the schools in Eretz Israel as part of an agreement with the Zionist Organization, under Rabbi Maimon's supervision. Secondly, he proposed the creation of a moshav, to be set up by Mizrachi activists, in a place near Jerusalem which is now known as Kiryat Anavim.

Maimon, who reportedly took the rejection of his proposals very hard, was bitterly disappointed and depressed as a result. Reines comforted him, advising him to continue fighting for religious influence from within the Zionist movement, and gave the younger man a vote of confidence by asking him to go to Russia to strengthen Mizrachi there.

By this time, Reines's health had steeply declined. He died on September 22, 1915, aged seventy-six.

Rabbi Abraham Isaac Hacohen Kook   הרב אברהם יצחק הכהן קוק

RABBI ABRAHAM ISAAC HACOHEN KOOK
(1865–1935)

RABBI KOOK was born into a family of Torah scholars in Latvia. His ancestors included several Torah scholars and adherents of both the Chassidic and Mitnaged schools of Jewish religious thought. Two great-grandfathers studied at the illustrious Volozhin Yeshiva, one of whom was a mystic who saw no conflict between the rational and mystical traditions of Torah study. In a move that predicted the future, he joined the Chabad Chasidic movement. This approach of tolerance and understanding came to define Kook's activities and writings.

Kook was educated partly at home under his father's guidance and partly in a traditional religious primary school (*cheder*), where he was an outstanding pupil. At thirteen years of age he went to the nearby town of Lotzin to study with Rabbi Yaakov Horowitz, a great-uncle who left a permanent impression on him, and in 1881 he returned to his parents' home where he came under the influence of Rabbi Reuben Halevi, a leading rabbi of the day and an avowed opponent of the pilpul style of Talmudic learning. Kook was apparently so outstanding in both intellect and character that Rabbi Halevi was heard to say that Kook was worthy of taking his place.[1]

In 1884 he was engaged to marry Batsheva, the daughter of Rabbi Eliyahu Dov Rabinowitz Teomim, who was known as the Aderet (a Hebrew acronym comprised of his four names). On his advice, Kook resumed his studies at Volozhin and is said to have spent eighteen hours a day learning. He was now called the Ilui from Ponevez, the city where his father-in-law served as rabbi, and shortly after joining the yeshiva he

---

[1] *The Encyclopedia of Religious Zionism,* vol. 5, 91.

received his rabbinic ordination from Rabbi Naftali Zvi Yehudah Berlin, the Netziv. His first work was a response to criticisms of the Netziv's commentary on the Chumash, *Ha'amek Davar.*

At the age of twenty he married and wrote a defense of traditional Judaism against the maskilim. At first the Netziv disapproved of these efforts since they took time away from Kook's Torah learning; but he withdrew his objection when he learned that Kook carried out the work together with associates. Kook used this platform to call upon all rabbis to unite despite their differences in order to make Torah understood and ensure that its laws were carried out. He also stressed the need to spread the knowledge of Aggadah as well as Halakhah.

Rabbi of Zeimelis and of Boisk

Many communities asked Rav Kook to become their rabbi. At first he refused, fearing that a full-time position would interfere with his studies, but changed his mind after the Chofetz Chaim persuaded him to accept the position of rabbi of Zeimelis in the Kovno area.

In Zeimelis, Kook's first task was to heal the rifts between various sections of the community. Because the town was small he was able to continue his learning and personal development, and published a book entitled *Abraham Yitzchok Kook on the Aggadot of the Rabbis.*

Kook's tenure in Zeimelis was marked by personal and communal difficulty. His wife, Batsheva, died, and the tragedy deepened his already considerable interest in mysticism (which he called "the hidden Torah"). At the same time, an epidemic threatened the town. In a dramatic show of leadership Kook stood up in the middle of Yom Kippur prayers and ate in full view of his community, thereby persuading his congregation to follow suit despite the traditional fast.

Already at this early stage in his life Kook showed an interest in all sectors of the community and a desire to achieve a modus vivendi between religious and secular groups that would enable them to live at peace within the same communal framework. To this end he prepared a plan that he believed would heal the rifts between the religious and the secular as well as between Hasidim and mitnagdim. Unfortunately, nothing came of it. Another indication of his concern for all segments of the community was his support of a project to publish a Talmud in one volume with basic comments for laypeople in the margin.

An interesting sidelight on Kook's character and capacity appears in his connection with the town of Boisk. His candidacy for the Boisk rabbinate was rejected on the unusual grounds that he was too righteous as well as too young. Nevertheless, when the incumbent rabbi left to live in Eretz Israel in 1895, Kook was appointed to replace him. The significance of the appointment was that the town comprised a cross section of all groups in the Diaspora – Hasidim, mitnagdim, Lithuanian scholars and secularists. Kook was already known for his ability to unite different sectors of a community and, as far as possible within Halacha, to tolerate differences in religious approach.

Kook was concerned not only with broad issues of common interest but also with the personal religious observance of the community's members; and when he discovered, in 1891, that some members of his community did not put on tefillin in accordance with the halacha, he anonymously published a book on the subject urging rabbis throughout Lithuania to address the problem.

As part of his concern for the overall education of communities, particularly young people, he formed the Tiferet Bachurim Society in 1892 in order to encourage them to study the Bible. He also established a library that was suited to their needs. Since at the time, studying the Bible outside the context of the Talmud and its commentaries was not considered of fundamental importance, the founding of this organization was revolutionary. It indicated Kook's concern for the community as a whole, young and old, those who were learned and those who were not.

During his years as the rabbi of Boisk and Zeimelis, Rabbi Kook published articles that showed he had already formed the ideas upon which he later expanded as chief rabbi in Eretz Israel. In particular, he denied that the mission of the Jews had ended and challenged the nation to rise to greater spiritual heights.

Kook wrote that there are two elements in the national consciousness: an innate, instinctive feeling of identification and belonging, and a specific essence of nationhood. An individual's connection to the collective is dominant in secular Jewish nationhood, he wrote, whereas the spiritual element that should characterize that nationhood was absent. The long exile so dimmed the national feelings of the people that they began to identify with other nations and assimilate. The nations' rejection made them reconsider their position, and since they were estranged from their faith, they found rest only in nationalism.[2]

However, Kook believed that the spiritual connection would be restored. "Through their national awakening, the Jewish people will be brought nearer to God," he wrote. "If the Zionist Organization awakens the people and succeeds in recreating our national condition and when the spirit of our people is raised to direct all its activities towards this noble goal, the true return of Israel, seeking God, will be in our hands."

Despite his implicit praise of secular nationalism, Kook did not spare the Zionists from criticism. Regarding the various nationalistic movements that sprouted during the nineteenth and twentieth centuries, he warned, "Nationalism not based on values of faith can degenerate into chauvinism."[3] At the same time, he called on the religious community to join the Zionists in order to become its ideological arbiter.[4] In private, he sometimes spoke or wrote in a different vein; referring to Zionist leader Max Nordau, a non-believer who was married to a non-Jew, as "that wicked man."[5] Kook's views on the relationship between secular and religious people in the Zionist movement became the ideological basis of Mizrachi.

When the position of chief rabbi of Jaffa became vacant in 1902, Kook found himself under pressure to refuse the appointment. In particular, Ze'ev Yaavetz (1847–1924), an outstanding writer within the Mizrachi Movement, wrote that Jaffa was an ungodly city and if Kook moved to Eretz Israel he would be better advised to take up a position in Petah Tikvah or Jerusalem. Rabbi Nussbaum warned him that he would encounter new conditions and problems in Jaffa arising out of the land itself and asked Kook whether he had any expertise in such problems.

---

[2] Maimon, *The History of the Rabbi* and *Essays of the Rabbi.* Jerusalem: 1937.
[3] *Encyclopedia of Religious Zionism*, 91–92.
[4] *Op. cit.,* 96–97.
[5] *Ibid.*

Kook replied that not only was he completely familiar with the relevant laws but as a *kohen,* he knew the laws relating to the priesthood.[6] Kook ultimately accepted the appointment, assuming the position in Jaffa in 1904.

A Eulogy for Herzl

When Theodor Herzl died two months after Kook took up his position in Jaffa, the latter delivered a public eulogy in which he expounded upon the two stages leading to redemption: the Messiah of the House of Joseph and the Messiah of the House of David. Kook said there were two streams in Jewry, one material (the body) and the other spiritual (the soul). He said that the former exists among all the nations while the latter exists only among the Jewish people. He likened the phenomenon of Zionism to the footsteps of the Messiah of the House of Joseph, saying that Herzl represented the slain Messiah of the House of Joseph, the lesson of which we are called upon to absorb. However, for some reason Kook did not mention Herzl by name.[7]

The General Press

Kook read the general Hebrew press and replied to an article by Eliezer Ben Yehudah, who had criticized the new yishuv for turning away from Judaism.[8] He called on young people to carry on Jewish tradition with pride and to ensure the continuation of its natural uniqueness which found expression in the Torah and Mitzvot. The old Yishuv rebuked him for even entering into discussion with non-believers.

Education

Over the years Kook expressed clear views on the content and style of Jewish education, particularly in his letters. He set the tone in an open letter to young people in 1905 in which he wrote, "All the strengths will develop, whether the source be from the Jewish people or from the best of the enlightened nations with which we have come into contact, and

---

[6] *Sichot ha-rabbi,* 302–303.
[7] *Maamarei ha-rabbi,* 94–99, and *Sinai* 47: 327–331.
[8] *Hashkafah,* 26 Adar I 5660 (1900).

when we preserve our own way of life we add strength according to our own character and true nature."[9]

His approach to education was not merely ideological, but also had practical significance for the development of the country. Kook planned to build vocational training facilities in order to train young people so that they could contribute the development of the economy while at the same time maintaining a "deep regard for the national assets of Judaism."[10] He bemoaned the lack of discipline in the old yishuv and criticized schools for failing to teach secular subjects. He said that schools needed well-constructed buildings and must impose discipline with high standards of behavior, and that schools must teach not only traditional religious subjects but also Jewish religious philosophy and thought, the general sciences and foreign languages.

He drew up a blueprint for a new style of yeshiva that was intended to attract students from all over the world. Its curriculum would include traditional Judaic studies, including Bible studies, Jewish thought and philosophy, alongside secular subjects.

Originally, Kook planned to build the new institution in Yavneh, the seat of learning established by Yochanan ben Zakkai immediately after the destruction of the Second Temple in the year 70 C.E. However, when he heard that the Hebrew University would be located in Jerusalem, he changed the proposed site to Jerusalem. It was unthinkable that the secular Hebrew University should be built in the Holy City while the projected yeshiva was located elsewhere. Nevertheless, Kook did not wish to abolish the traditional yeshiva, which he considered to be an insurance against secularism, although he doubted whether it would survive.[11]

One focus of Kook's new yeshiva was to train rabbis competent both in rabbinical and secular disciplines who could meet the spiritual needs of the yishuv community and, where possible, could serve as rabbis of the settlements. The syllabus included Bible and Talmud studies, midrash, mysticism, ethics, grammar and religious poetry.

---

[9] *Letters,* vol 1, 16–19.
[10] *Ibid.,* vol. 2, 148.
[11] *Letters,* 206, 260–261.

Evolution

Kook realized the challenge presented by Darwin's theory of evolution to traditional views of the universe and humankind, and discussed the problem at some length in a letter that he wrote in 1904. After pointing out that some Jewish commentators conceived of God's building and destroying worlds, he argued that it was not necessary to consider any such ideas as to be accepted or rejected. The biblical narrative, he said, was obscure in its description about the origins of the universe. According to the Midrash, the written creation story is impossible to understand literally, and the text therefore simply states that in the beginning God created heaven and earth. Therefore, there was no contradiction between the Torah and scientific theory.

In any event, Kook believed that even if Darwin's theory was correct, the process was ultimately directed by God. His views on the subject are an interesting echo of those expressed by Pierre Teilhard de Chardin (1881–1955), the Jesuit priest and paleontologist who accepted Darwin's theories with the fundamental qualification that the evolution from the most primitive form of life to man was divinely directed.

Furthermore, Kook was open to the possibility that further developments in science might prove or disprove Darwin's theory. He wrote that the purpose of the Torah was not to give all the facts, but rather to teach us the intrinsic meaning of creation and the development of humanity.

Kook and the Settlements

Kook was deeply concerned that Torah should be part of life in each settlement. For this purpose, he drafted a plan to appoint rabbis who would act as religious advisers.

Kook knew that many young people in the Yishuv regarded the old "shtetl Jew" as an anachronism, and he understood that new rabbis would have to understand the new style of living characteristic of the kibbutz and moshav in order to minister appropriately to their needs. He wrote, "The courage, with the knowledge and natural pride that prevail in the new Yishuv, cannot bear the bent back, the blushing and sad faces that reflect fear and weakness of heart, the shifting eyes that showed despair, the foreign eastern clothing, combined with grinding poverty."[12]

In an attempt to draw the religious establishment nearer to secular settlements Kook organized a group of rabbis to tour the country and assess the religious situation for themselves. He hoped that in this way they would be able to persuade the settlers to observe the mitzvot. Kook himself led the group, which achieved mixed results at best, and it is doubtful whether any substantial success was achieved in increasing religious observance. The experiment was never repeated.

Kook and the Sabbatical Year

While Kook was still the chief rabbi of Jaffa, he had to deal with the severe problems posed by observance of the sabbatical year, when working the land is forbidden. Farmers in the nascent Yishuv faced bankruptcy and starvation if they had to close their operations for a year. Had the problem not been resolved amicably, the consequences would have been disastrous.

With great courage, Kook allowed work to be carried out on the settlements during that year on the basis of the sale of the land to a non-Jew. He stressed the provisional nature of the dispensation, which was designed to ensure the survival of the pioneers, writing: "In view of the dire poverty of Eretz Israel's inhabitants, we are constrained to resort to this ad-hoc measure." Although Kook was subjected to harsh criticism for authorizing the sale, which is known in Hebrew as the heter mechira, he refused to change his ruling and in this respect would not submit to the Jerusalem rabbinate. He wrote at the time in terms indicating his closeness to the settlements and involvement in their problems: "I am steeped in the affairs of the settlers whether I wish it or not. This enables me to assess their problems more effectively than the rabbis of Jerusalem, who are distant from them both geographically and mentally. I am distressed by the unexpected challenge to my shemitta ruling…. I had no alternative…. I was solely concerned with the building of our holy land."

---

[12] *Letters* 4.1, 195.

Kook and Eretz Israel

For Kook, the Land of Israel had inherent sanctity. Accordingly, he believed that living in Eretz Israel, acquiring land there and developing its soil for agriculture is the highest degree of religious observance. When Mizrachi leaders failed to convince the Jewish National Fund to observe the Sabbath on an institutional level, Kook told them categorically that land acquisition was a halachic imperative "whose weight equals that of all other the biblical precepts." Accordingly, because the Jewish National Fund's land purchases carried out the Divinely-ordained acquisition of Israel by the Jewish people in a way that precluded the need for war and loss of human life, such activities fell under the halachic category of *pikuach nefesh*, or saving lives, which overrides almost all other commandments, including Sabbath observance. Not even the desecration of the Sabbath could diminish support for the acquisition of land in Eretz Israel.

Kook insisted that the halacha in relation to work on the land should be observed strictly. Land must not be worked on the Sabbath, casks of wine must not be carried by non-Jews and the use of Arab instead of Jewish labor on the Sabbath was forbidden. In general, Kook tried to bring education in the settlements in line with the spirit of the Torah. In order to increase his influence, he took part in fixing school syllabi and seeking capable teachers.

Kook, the Zionists and Mizrachi

Kook was necessarily involved in considering the place of religion in Zionism. In a letter to the St. Louis branch of Mizrachi, he wrote that while supporting Zionism and its general aims, Mizrachi must fight the proposal put forward by the Zionist leadership that Zionism should have nothing to do with religion. Although Kook planned to attend the Eleventh Zionist Congress in Vienna, Arab riots made it necessary for him to remain in the country. Since Kook realized the importance of establishing more religious settlements, he urged Mizrachi to buy land in Yavneh in order to build a high-quality yeshiva there that would draw its inspiration from the Yavneh of old.

Although Kook had a close relationship with Mizrachi – he made it clear that he supported its aims and participated in its conferences – he never made his connection with the movement official. This was probably a wise decision since a close association with a political party would have weakened his relationship to and influence upon the Yishuv as a whole.

The Balfour Declaration and the Creation of the Chief Rabbinate

Several months after the beginning of World War I (1914–1918), Kook pushed for the establishment of diplomatic ties with the Great Powers regarding the status of Eretz Israel. Kook was in Europe when the war broke out, and was forced to spend the war years there. During that time, he envisaged a post-war peace conference that would deal with the position of Palestine, among other matters. He knew that Zionists in London were working through their government contacts to ensure the best possible outcome for the Yishuv, and Kook was realistic enough to understand that rabbis would have no significant role in this process.

The League of Nations gave the mandate to administer Palestine to Great Britain, whose policy was set out in the Balfour Declaration of 1918, which stipulated that a national home for the Jewish people should be established there, subject to the protection of the religious and civil rights of other segments of the population.

Kook regarded the Declaration as an important step towards the Jewish people's ultimate redemption. Regarding religion under the British Mandate, First High Commissioner Sir Herbert Samuel, and Attorney General Norman Bentwich considered the authority of the religious courts and eventually recommended that religious matters concerning the Jewish population should be decided by one authority in which Ashkenazim and the Sefardim would have equal representation. The body would have two presidents, one from the Ashkenazi community and one appointed by the Sefardim, and Kook insisted that each of them would be bear the title of Chief Rabbi. The committee that elected the chief rabbis would comprise two-thirds rabbis and one-third laymen.

There was considerable opposition to establishing a chief rabbinate, particularly on the part of the old Yishuv and communities outside

Palestine. Rabbi Diskin, an outstanding figure in the Haredi community, strongly opposed the new arrangements. Kook wrote to the opponents in moderate terms, stressing that the overriding consideration of the rabbis who supported the new structure was to strengthen religious life in the country.[13]

Kook believed the new structure represented a step towards reviving the authority of the Torah, comparable to the founding of the ancient academy at Yavneh by Rabbi Yochanan ben Zakkai. He was prepared to accept the inclusion of laymen, but only on condition that they act as advisers only. Day-to-day matters would be dealt with by a twenty–three-member executive analogous to the "little Sanhedrin" in ben Zakkai's time. Characteristically, Kook refrained from attacking those who opposed the new structure and called for tolerant, respectful disagreement.

Kook was not satisfied with a formal status for the Chief Rabbinate, which he felt must have the power to bind Jewish communities in the country. He also wanted to ensure that the local rabbinates and the rabbinical courts would have the authority to provide religious services for the population. The discussions on this matter took seven years. In the end it was decided that the rabbinate's budget would be subject to the elected body representing the whole Yishuv known as the Vaad ha-Leumi (the National Council) which was secular by definition. Although Kook was disappointed that the arrangement did not give the rabbis the decisive voice he had hoped for, he refused to bow to pressure from other religious groups to withdraw from the organized community.

He was not depressed by the war. On the contrary, "when there is a great war in the world, the strength of the Messiah arises."[14] He cited a reference in the traditional morning prayers to God as "Sovereign of Worlds," which goes on to describe Him as the One who renews the work of creation and ending with the hope that He will make a new light to shine on Zion.

---

[13] *Ha-makor,* vol. 2, 82, and op. cit. 256.
[14] *Orot,* 11.

Kook in London

During World War I, when Kook could not leave Europe, he accepted the position of rabbi of the Machzikei Hadass community in London. Before accepting the post, he asked the following questions:

1. Would his appointment be accepted without any dispute?
2. What tasks was he expected to undertake?
3. What was the relationship of the Machzikei Hadass to the British Chief Rabbi in general and how did the latter regard the proposed appointment?
4. What was the relationship of Rabbi Jung of the Adath Yisrael community to the Machzikei Hadass, which Jung had served as rabbi?[15]

Kook's relationship to the community's chief rabbi and lay leaders was strained during this period mainly because he did not understand the fundamental difference between the organization of the Anglo-Jewish community and that of communities in Eastern Europe. Following an unfortunate episode in which he issued a certificate to two young men confirming that they were yeshiva students and should therefore be exempt from military service, he was interrogated by the police as to the certificates' authenticity. It turned out that one of the young men had never studied in yeshiva at all.

When Kook explained that he had relied on information from the president of a synagogue where the young man worshipped, he was released with a warning. He did not realize that in England, matters such as this were dealt with only by the chief rabbi and lay leaders and that local rabbis were expected to seek advice before taking action.

The Jewish Brigade

Although Kook was enthusiastic about the formation of the Jewish Brigade, which Rav Kook said "bore the flag of the first flowering of our salvation,"[16] he expressed concern about religious standards of Brigade members. He stressed the need to observe kashrut, Shabbat and the

---

[15] *Letters,* vol. 1, 54–55.
[16] *Ibid.,* vol. 3, 134.

festivals, and avoided the problem of work on Shabbat by advising the Brigade to arrange for non-Jews to carry out any forbidden types of work that needed to be done on that day.[17]

Kook and the Non-Religious Settlements

Kook made strenuous efforts to influence the non-religious settlements, occasionally criticizing their lack of observance. For example, in Zichron Ya'akov he demanded that the bima, or reader's table, in a synagogue be moved from a place adjoining the Ark to the center of the sanctuary, and he strongly criticized the lack of religious content in the school curricula.

The settlers of secular communities resented Kook's visits, which produced no practical results. Nevertheless, Kook believed that by continued personal contact and by the power of the printed word, neither of which had been widely used before, the rabbis and religious settlers would be able to influence the non-religious population and in time persuade them to increase their level of observance. He particularly felt that explaining the spirituality inherent in the mitzvot would achieve this result.

Consistent with these views, Kook founded a movement, Degel Yerushalayim, whose purpose was to penetrate the Zionist Organization, convince it of the importance of religion in its activities and settlements and encourage religious elements in the Mizrachi Movement. Kook did not realize that Mizrachi might regard Degel Yerushalayim as a potential rival, which it did, and as a result the new organization disintegrated.

Despite his identification with and encouragement of the work of secular settlements, Kook met with little success in his attempts to encourage Sabbath observance. However, he did succeed in accomplishing two things: he was able to persuade Meir Dizengoff, the mayor of Tel Aviv, to close all municipal offices and undertakings on the Sabbath, and he was also able to obtain from Sir Ronald Storrs, the Governor of Jerusalem, a promise that where a local community had issued a regulation that the Sabbath must be publicly observed, violations would carry a penalty.[18]

---

[17] *Op. cit.,* 17.
[18] *Encyclopedia of Religious Zionism,* 294.

However, such victories were the exception rather than the rule. Kook's letter of protest requesting that the Thirteenth Zionist Congress and the Jewish National Fund not operate on the Sabbath met with rejection.

After his return to Eretz Israel following World War I, Kook embarked on a tour of the settlements together with the Rishon le-Zion, Rabbi Yaakov Meir, and Rabbi Barchov in order to observe changes that had occurred in religious observance. In a meeting with journalists after the tour, Kook said he found conditions in the settlements much improved since his previous visit before the war, but said that while the Zionist pioneers "had returned to our national foundation, they had not returned to our religious foundation." However, he added that the two were intertwined and eventually they would return to the religious foundation.[19]

Kook and the Chief Rabbinate of Jerusalem

On Kook's return to Palestine after World War I, Rabbi Zvi Pesah Frank (1873–1961) invited him to become the chief rabbi of Jerusalem. Religious matters in the city were in a state of chaos at the time – members of the rabbinical court had not even been paid – as a result of difficult economic conditions of the war years, and a council of rabbis was set up to bring order to the local rabbinate and to appoint a chief rabbi for the city.

However, the municipal council hesitated to make the appointment because they believed that the city's general difficulties must be resolved before a new chief rabbi took office. Despite the opposition, communal leaders met in Hebron and decided to offer Kook the position. Kook accepted on condition that his appointment have the support of the rabbis in the other holy cities – Safed, Tiberias and Hebron – and that the views of the Sefardim and rabbis and communities outside Palestine be sought.[20]

Although on his appointment Kook immediately set up a General Council of Rabbis of Eretz Israel, opposition continued. Opponents

---

[19] *Encyclopedia of Religious Zionism,* 344–345.
[20] See *Igrot,* vol. 3, 229, and *The Encyclopedia of Religious Zionism,* 201 and 301.

criticized him on the grounds that, among other things, he had not been appointed by the decision of the community as a whole, the official rabbinical court had not signed the letter of appointment, he lacked Torah knowledge and he was not sufficiently God-fearing. Significantly, one letter added, "Most fundamentally, he is not a rabbi of the old generation but rather an 'enlightened' rabbi of the new generation, a nationalist rabbi. Some say that his religion and nationalism are intertwined, while others say that his nationalism comes first and leads him to God and his religious faith." They also criticized his statement that he would be involved with places other than Jerusalem.[21]

Women's Suffrage

In Kook's view, since the Jewish claim to Eretz Israel was based on religious principles, it followed that all decisions made by the Yishuv must accord with religious tradition. Therefore – according to his interpretation of Jewish tradition – because women were forbidden to participate in public affairs, they could neither vote nor hold office.

Rabbi Judah Maimon, the leader of Mizrachi, took the unprecedented step of disregarding Kook's views even though they reflected rabbinical opinion in the country. In order not to appear guilty of flouting the chief rabbinate's authority, Maimon treated Kook's statement as a non-binding expression of opinion rather than as a halachic decision. There appears to have been no further discussion on this matter, and women participated in the elections as voters and candidates without further opposition.[22]

There is little doubt that had Kook persisted in his objection to women's suffrage, his relationship with non-religious elements in the Yishuv would have been severely damaged and his influence in the country jeopardized. Although the dispute over women's rights in this respect persisted over the years, Kook made no further statements on the matter. He also knew that issuing a ban would only result in divisiveness. When members of Mizrachi asked whether they should boycott elections that were open to women, Kook urged them not to do so, though he repeated his opinion that women should not hold public office.

---

21 *The Encyclopedia of Religious Zionism,* 238.
22 *Op. cit.,* 232–234.

Many rabbis criticized him for not taking a stronger line against the election of women. There was even a move to replace him as chief rabbi in new elections, though the suggestion faltered because British authorities took no action on the proposal.

The Western Wall

Kook waged an ongoing battle for Jewish rights at the Western Wall and was frequently in dispute with British authorities, as well as with the Arabs and their leader, the Grand Mufti of Jerusalem. Kook demanded that the High Commissioner transfer the site, which was under Muslim control, to Jewish supervision. In order to make his position clearer, he referred to the Western Wall in an article as "our wall" even though Arabs frequently attacked Jews near the Wall and the governor of Jerusalem demanded that Jews not light lamps there on Friday evenings. Upon Kook's protest the ban on lamps was rescinded, and as a result of Kook's efforts the British government, as part of its White Paper on the subject, reiterated the status quo, which confirmed Jewish rights to worship at the Western Wall, although it would remain under Muslim control.

Nevertheless, disturbances at the Western Wall continued. Arab workers even began to demolish a structure adjacent to it and Kook wrote to the Governor of Jerusalem demanding that this work be stopped. In response, he was told that the governor would only stop the work if it disturbed the worshippers at the Wall itself, to which Kook replied that Arabs deliberately passed by with laden donkeys in order to disturb worshippers. Worse, on the ninth day of the Hebrew month of Av, a day of national mourning over the destruction of both Temples in Jerusalem, two thousand Arabs descended on the Wall and disturbed the worshippers while in other parts of the country they rioted, killing dozens of Jews. Yitzchak ben Zvi, the chairman of the representative body of the Jewish community, walked to Kook's home on the Sabbath to tell him what had happened. Kook fainted at the news.

Although it was the Sabbath, Kook immediately telephoned the First Secretary of the Mandatory Power, demanding that the disturbances be stopped. Incredibly, the latter replied that he did not know what he could do as he had no orders from above to restrain the rioters. Kook lost his temper and said to the First Secretary, "To save innocent citizens from murderers who are attacking them you need an order from above?! I give you the order. In the name of human conscience I demand that you fulfill your obligations and defend the lives of Jewish citizens in this country!"[23]

Upon the High Commissioner's return to Palestine, Kook criticized him for remaining absent at such a time and demanded that he disarm the Arabs. The reply was that if the Arabs were disarmed, the Jews would have to be disarmed as well. To no avail, Kook pointed out that while the Arabs used arms to attack Jews, the Jews bore arms in self-defense.

After the disturbances Kook wrote an article of encouragement to the Yishuv asking people not to give way to pessimism. He said that those who followed the Yishuv's progress would realize that after every setback, the country went into a more intensive phase of development and that the losses that the Yishuv suffered would lead to "the light that would be revealed."[24]

Kook not only demanded unimpeded access to the Wall, but also pressed for elementary amenities that had been prohibited under pressure from the Mufti, including the right to bring small folding chairs there, to blow the shofar on Rosh Hashana and Yom Kippur, and to light the area with torches. Kook also had to negotiate on the question of bringing lulavim to the Wall during the Succot holiday. This was eventually permitted, although reading the Torah during the intermediate days of the Festival was forbidden.

As a general rule, Kook did not compromise on Jewish rights. Under no circumstances would he agree to a suggestion that the visits of Jews to the Wall be temporarily suspended. When the British government proposed at the League of Nations that the Wall be under Arab control subject to the rights of the Jews to approach it, Kook advised the chairman of the national committee to reject the proposal out of hand, since in his view the Jews had no right to surrender the Wall.[25]

---

[23] *Op. cit.,* 356–357.
[24] *Keriot gedolot,* 79–80; op. cit. 358.
[25] M.T. Neriya, *Moadei ha-rabbi,* 477. *Op. cit.,* 314.

University Education

Kook was ambivalent about the establishment of the Hebrew University. He asked Chaim Weizmann to prevent the teaching of academic criticism of the Bible, and his speech at the opening of the University reflected his hopes and doubts. He defined the University's purpose as publicizing the values and concepts of Judaism while at the same time including in its syllabi general knowledge obtained from humanity as a whole, adapting the best of the latter for the benefit of the Jewish people.[26] He clearly did not understand the concept underlying a university: that it must be open to all ideas and not be bound by any particular tradition.

To some extent, Kook's views about Hebrew University prefigured the ideological basis of Bar Ilan University, founded in 1956 near Tel Aviv, in an attempt to combine traditional Jewish teachings and values with the freedom of thought that is the mark of a university.

Repentance (Teshuva)

Kook's views on repentance appear in his work *Orot ha-teshuva*. In this work, he deals with the repentance of the individual of Israel and of the world. For Kook, the origin of teshuva is the longing of individuals to be purer than they are. However, in Kook's view individuals are not alone; they are part of a people engaged in the process of teshuva and therefore are partly responsible for *tikkun ha-am* (national reform). Kook saw repentance as a joy and said that the greater the effort required to repent, the greater the joy when repentance is effective. He rejected the commonly-held view that teshuva leads to feelings of deep regret, saying that the pain felt during the process of repentance stemmed from the fact that the evil part of the human essence must be uprooted.

As Alkalai and Kalischer had done before him, Kook linked teshuva with Israel's redemption, seeing "the revival of the people as the basis for building the great repentance and the repentance of the whole world that will come after it." He seems to have regarded the nascent state of Israel

---

[26] *The Encyclopedia of Religious Zionism*, 322.

as a nation as its first step towards repentance which in turn would lead to redemption.[27]

National and Universal – Holy and Secular

Kook regarded secular Zionism as fundamentally flawed in its neglect of the need for moral-religious regeneration. However, even in secular Zionism he saw the seeds of a reversion to "Judaism's radiant and sublime inward concept." Zionists, even subconsciously, drew on the divine source of national Jewish ideals and should not be condemned. He wrote, "The Jewish national concept is inherently sacred and exalted.... Let us infuse it with a truly enlightened religious spirit."[28]

Consequently, Kook believed that it was a mistake to separate nationality and religion. "In all matters of thought feeling and ideals we find in the Israelite nation one indivisible unit which together comprise its unique form," he said.

Kook was more specific regarding the combination of the holy and the secular in the nation's rebirth.

> We believe... that in everything that helps in the building of the land and strengthening the nation there is the hidden word of God for the rebirth of the sacred and of the Holy Land. Therefore, we have not separated ourselves from any party... from which the awakening comes. From the day on which the practical dream of building the land began to be realized, there was concern to strengthen the spiritual vision and breathe the holy fire into the secular because Israel's deliverance cannot succeed without the blending of the sacred and the secular.[29]

Kook felt that every nation wishing to survive must comprise elements of the sacred, the national and the universal. He applied this to political life in Palestine, writing: "The Orthodox carry the banner of the sacred, the nationalists fight for national aspirations and the liberals are the universal element in culture ethics and so on." He maintained that all

---

[27] See *Orot ha-teshuva*, 122; *Op. cit.*, 322.
[28] See Yaron, *The Philosophy of Rabbi Kook*, 202–203.
[29] *Ma'amarei ha-Reiyah*, 257–259.

three are necessary for a healthy nation to survive. Similarly, each nation has its own talents, and ultimately all the talents will combine for the benefit of humanity when "God becomes Ruler over all the earth; on that day God shall be one and His Name one."

The Land of Israel

For Kook the essence of the Jewish people is rooted in the laws of the Torah and the Torah is primarily of the Land of Israel. This identification, unique among the nations, differs from the affection of other peoples for their land that mirrors a drawn-out historical process beginning with the settlement of masses of people in a particular area which generates a sense of identity. In Kook's view, Israel was unique in that its attachment to the land developed even before they entered it, inspired by the transcendental and celestial in the hearts of sojourners (i.e., the Patriarchs and Matriarchs) whose origin was divine, with no natural basis.

Consequently, for Kook the purchase of land in Eretz Israel is a halachic imperative "whose importance equals that of all the biblical precepts." He accordingly refused to advise the Mizrachi organization to boycott the Jewish National Fund over the latter's failure to ensure Sabbath observance, saying that the actions of certain settlers on Jewish National Fund property did not exempt Mizrachi from continuing its sacred involvement in land acquisition.[30]

Judaism and the Diaspora

Despite his insistence on the centrality of the Land of Israel to the Jewish people, Kook did not minimize the importance of the Jewish experience in exile. He wrote:

> When we interacted with our neighbor nations we absorbed their foreign spirit which, however, could not be assimilated and proved to be our adversary.... [W]e have been purified in the melting pot of poverty; during its two-thousand-year duration... we had no relationship with material things. We were a nation

---

[30] *Hazon ha-geulah*, 221–223.

floating in the air, dreaming only of the Kingdom of Heaven....
Now we are called upon to materialize this longing in life. This is
the renaissance. This renaissance accumulates all our eternal
ideals... in the attempt of generations to return to the Land
where our rights and gifts await us, in a respectful relationship to
the whole of our past heritage and a lofty spirit towards the future
elevation of the nation which ascends according to our desire and
work. The historic love for the people and the land must be
nourished by the beliefs and opinions of the past.

This evaluation of the Diaspora as having a positive spiritual role in
the history of the Jewish people contrasts dramatically with the thinking
of mainstream Zionism, which saw the history of Diaspora Jewry as a
"martyrology" (the term used by the historian Lewis Namier).

Judaism and Other Cultures

Kook contrasts the relationship between Judaism and other cultures in
exile, when "restriction became necessary" and any thought that did not
develop wholly within the camp of Israel could subvert Israel's faith, with
life "in an era in which Israel's strength is great and its soul shines in
holiness, with unity and blessing with Temple prophecy and wisdom...
when expansion towards secular interests and in particular towards
knowledge of the lives of other nations and peoples and their literatures
is beneficial."

In another passage Kook went further in proposing acceptance of
other cultures, provided that those contributions are consistent with
Jewish values. He said that "in this way we will be able to strengthen our
traditions, but only when the Jewish people is in its own land."[31]

Nevertheless, beyond this diversity there is a principle of
"transcendental unity" expressed in God's sovereignty of which Judaism
is the center as the quintessence of humanity, so that Israel alone is
graced with the divine facility "that embraces the totality of the human
being."[32]

---

[31] *Igrot,* vol 1, 56.
[32] *Igrot ha-Re'iyah,* vol 1, 175, and Yaron, 246.

The Righteous and the Wicked

Kook asserts that the foundation of righteousness in every generation is also supported by the wicked, "who, with all their wickedness, as long as they cling with their heart's desire to the collectivity of a nation," are the ones referred to in the verse "Your people are righteous." In accordance with this view and applying it to the Yishuv, Kook asserts that the national home will create "a mighty spirit" in which the soul of the nation will be reawakened to "establish the faith of the Lord God of Israel in the world."

Kook compared the weakness of Jewish life in the Diaspora, which prevents the pride of faith from appearing in the world, to the inner power that will break out and assume its authentic form in Eretz Israel. He warned, however, that "assertion of national enthusiasm without a spiritual basis" will remain "only a shadow of life."

Kook elaborated upon the necessary connection between Torah and the return to Zion, asserting that without the strength of Torah to broaden the nation's soul, the inner demand of return to Zion is not aroused with the necessary faith.

Summary

Kook was educated exclusively in traditional yeshivot in which the curriculum was confined to Talmud and its commentaries. As we have seen, he was quickly recognized as an *ilui* (prodigy). Nothing in his formative years presaged either the breadth of interests he showed as a communal rabbi or his innovations in thought and action in the application of Orthodox Judaism to the daily life of a self-governing Jewish community in its own land. He was the only one of the pioneers of religious Zionism who lived in Eretz Israel (with the exception of Alkalai, who retired and spent his last years there), and the only one who dealt with the day-to-day problems of the Yishuv.

Kook was exceptional in reaching out to the secular settlements and population in an attempt to introduce a religious element into their lives. His views on secular Zionists and non-religious elements in Eretz Israel were revolutionary. He viewed settling and developing the land as a halachic imperative equal to all the other commandments. In his opinion, this obligation was so vital that those who carried it out, though they might deny it, were imbued with the spirit of Judaism. Accordingly, he encouraged the Mizrachi Organization to remain part of the Zionist Organization in order to bring religious influence to bear on its activities.

Kook's philosophy rejected the idea of complete separation between religious and secular and between the spiritual and material worlds, since every institution or material thing contains a spiritual element. This holistic view of society and material things enabled him to relate to all sections of the Yishuv sympathetically, and he carried these ideas even further, antagonizing a large part of the Orthodox community by declaring that those who lived and settled in Eretz Israel but kept none of the commandments were more worthy than those who observed all the commandments but lived in the Diaspora.

In modern terms one could describe Kook as an extreme religious nationalist. Although this statement is true, it is incomplete for two reasons. First, he felt that the Jewish people should absorb those ideas from non-Jewish nations that are compatible with Judaism (though apparently only after they are living in Eretz Israel). Second, he looked forward to the time when all nations, each with its own particular talents, would unite and accept the yoke of the kingdom of God as set forth in the Aleinu prayer in the traditional Jewish liturgy, which quotes the prophecy that "on that day God will be One and His name One."

Like his predecessors Alkalai, Kalischer, Mohliver and Reines, Kook appears to have underestimated the depth of Arab hostility to Zionism, which found especially violent expression in the riots of 1929. He was primarily the thinker and theologian whose writings and opinions reinterpreted the concept of religious Zionism for the twentieth century. In addition to his involvement in the practical affairs of the Yishuv, he placed religious Zionism and religious thought at the center of Jewish life, inspiring generations of traditional Jewish pioneers.

Rabbi Yehudah Leib Maimon (Fishman)   הרב יהודה לייב הכהן מימון (פישמן)

Rabbi Yehudah Leib Maimon (Fishman) (1875–1962)

Rabbi Yehudah Leib was the son of Avraham Elimelech, who studied in the *bet midrash* of the Vilna Gaon. When Russian authorities insisted that the family adopt a surname, Avraham Elimelech chose Maimon. However, the change did not satisfy the authorities and Elimelech adopted the surname Fishman, which apparently was acceptable.

As a child, Yehudah Leib studied with the best teachers in Bessarabia. He soon displayed his considerable intellectual gifts, pointing out difficulties and asking challenging questions. By the age of eleven he was known as a scholar, and by the age of thirteen he had learned the entire Talmud. This was a remarkable achievement, particularly given his exceptionally poor eyesight, which plagued him throughout his life.

Maimon was well-read in a wide variety of subjects, including Halacha, Kabbala, Aggada, Jewish philosophy and secular literature. He wrote widely about the history of halacha and the development of religious Zionistic thought. Characteristic of his writings were his expertise in Jewish literature through the ages, scientific theory, and general rules for Torah study. He also wrote an explanation of halacha and the basis of Zionist thought.

His works were not intended merely as writings but rather as the basis for dealing with practical problems. He also wrote at length about Maimonides and the Vilna Gaon – not only about their personalities but also about their environments. He wrote particularly about the sources on which Maimonides drew – a basic text today for all who wish to understand Maimonides's writings. He also published a revised edition of Maimonides's halachic work *Mishneh Torah,* as well as a six-volume biography of several influential Torah scholars.

Maimon began his career in community activism at an early age. He was active in communal affairs, founding societies for the study Mishna, the purchase of books, to provide employment for the poor and wood to heat their houses in the winter and more. These activities presaged his later intellectual and social interests.

Around this time, movements such as Chovevei Zion and the Bilu (an acronym of *Bet Ya'akov, lekhu ve-nelkha* – "House of Jacob, come let us go") Student Society emerged to encourage aliyah. Maimon's father instilled in him a love for Eretz Israel through the writings of Tzvi Hirsch Kalischer; members of Chovevei Zion were frequent visitors in the family home, and he was also influenced by the work *Hibbat Zion,* written by Rabbi Yitzhak Yaakov Reines.

At the age of sixteen Maimon went to study in a yeshiva in Latvia, but consulted with Rabbi Samuel Mohliver before interrupting his work on behalf of Zionism. Mohliver advised him to study before resuming his work for the movement, and Maimon studied with some of the great rabbinic figures of the time in Vilna, Kovno, Seravnic and Vilki. At the same time, he continued his work for Chovevei Zion, and in writing of his admiration for Theodor Herzl stated that he, Maimon, had cherished the dream of a Jewish state for much of his life.

Maimon's Zionism led him away from the rabbinate. He feared that he would have to give in to communal authorities and other Orthodox leaders who disapproved of his ideas, particularly on the primacy of settling in Eretz Israel and of Zionism. He turned down rabbinical positions in Russian Galicia and in Great Britain to become a magid (preacher) in his birthplace, and his sermons made a considerable impression on the community. Aside from traditional halacha and specifically religious matters, his speeches covered a variety of subjects, including religious nationalism and Zionism. His influence spread beyond his hometown, and in particular he made links between towns in Bessarabia and the center of the Zionist Movement.

Apart from Herzl, Maimon was also influenced by Rabbi Jacob Reines and the Mizrachi Organization. Maimon and Reines became close friends, cementing their relationship during the struggle to prevent the

Zionist Movement from entering the field of culture. When the World Zionist Organization resolved to undertake cultural work over the objections of Mizrachi, Maimon and Reines led the fight within Mizrachi to remain inside the Zionist movement in order to continue the struggle from within.

The Mizrachi Conference in Krakow, 1903

This conference was called in order to unite all religious organizations in supporting the Yishuv. Maimon was re-elected to the World Center and although he pressed for such support, his attempt to bring in Agudat Israel failed. Fiercely critical of the secular leadership, he called for efforts to stop the Zionist Organization from discriminating against religious groups, for public observance of Shabbat, festivals and kashrut in official institutions, and for an effort to increase aliyah. Strikingly, he said that the permanent danger to Judaism was not heresy but ignorance, which would only be reduced by Torah study.

Maimon's speech at the conference was outstanding. In 1904, he was elected to the World Center of the Movement and to the various committees that dealt with the party's by laws, publicity, literature and education.

In 1905 he accepted the position of Rabbi in Ungani, a town on the Bessarabian border. He immediately gained respect and love from the Jewish community and from non-Jews who sometimes asked him to arbitrate disputes instead of going to the civil court. His influence and acceptance by non-Jews helped to spare local Jews the pogroms that afflicted other parts of the country.

In Ungani he founded a religious Zionist society which he called Achvah (friendship), whose constitution obligated members to settle in Israel permanently within the next ten years. Some of its members met this condition.

During his term of office in the rabbinate, Maimon continued his work for Zionism and attended Zionist Congresses. Meanwhile, other communities became interested in him as a rabbi, but the Ungani community persuaded him to remain with them. During this period he founded the monthly *Ha-yonah* journal for literary and Talmudic writings.

In 1908 and 1911, Maimon visited Eretz Israel on behalf of Mizrachi in order to examine the possibilities of religious cultural work. He visited again in 1911, and on both visits he considered the possibilities for Mizrachi. However, even at this early stage, his interest in the Yishuv as a whole was evident. While he was in Eretz Israel he became familiar with all aspects of life in the country, social, educational and religious, eventually becoming an important source of information for all those who wished to learn about the country. He was especially interested in the Tachkemoni religious school and persuaded Mizrachi in Russia to take an active interest in it.

During this period he was imprisoned by the Russian authorities several times for possessing Zionist literature, all of which was confiscated.

When the Tenth Zionist Congress approved the Zionist Organization's involvement with "cultural activities" over the Mizrachi delegates' objections, Maimon joined Reines in recommending that they remain inside the organization and criticized those who left the Zionist Movement:

> Some of us almost expected to be lynched after it became known in extremist Chassidic circles that we remained within Zionism even after "the Mizrachists" of Frankfurt left it, pronouncing it a "*shmata.*" However, the hearts of all of these [Mizrachists] yearned for the general national rebirth in all its streams and parties. Because we desired so strongly to be partners in rebuilding the land and in the revival of our national home, we agreed, with inner pain and deep sorrow and pounding hearts, to continue the work with the war.[1]

Ha-tor

In 1921 Maimon founded *Ha-tor,* a weekly newspaper that was published for fifteen years, of which he was the editor for twelve. It was here that Mizrachi's motto, "The land of Israel for the people of Israel according to the Torah of Israel," first appeared.

---

[1] *Op. cit.,* 29.

The paper's first editorial set forth its two-fold aim: to provide an outlet for literary prose, poetry, discussions on Jewish thought, research on the Land of Israel and development of the Hebrew language; and to deal with the problems of the country as a whole, as well as those of individual cities and villages. Ha-tor also wished to serve as a source of knowledge for Mizrachi regarding Diaspora Jewry, and would deal with political life and world events with a focus on the Diaspora. The publication became one of the pillars of the Mizrachi Movement.

The Balfour Declaration and the Chief Rabbinate

When World War I broke out in 1914, Maimon and other Zionist leaders, including David Ben-Gurion and Yitzhak Ben-Zvi, were imprisoned by the Turkish authorities. When Maimon was asked to name other Zionist leaders under threat of death, he refused – an early example of the courage he showed throughout his life. The group was subsequently banished to the United States, where they spent the war years. After the war, Maimon returned to Palestine on the first available ship.

As the leader of Mizrachi, Maimon played a crucial role in the establishment of the chief rabbinate. In 1917, when the British Government stated its support for the establishment of a national home for the Jewish People in Palestine in the Balfour Declaration, it became clear to Maimon that this ought to lead to the adoption of halacha as the law of Eretz Israel. He said that this would also be a natural development from the Mandate itself.

Maimon used the occasion of the Balfour Declaration to convene a conference of Mizrachi, where he was put in charge of practical work in Palestine. Characteristically, he criticized the organization for diverting almost all its work to the branches in the United States and hardly any to developing the religious Yishuv in Palestine, and he worked hard to secure support for directing money to religious settlements and the establishment of a network of religious schools in Israel, as well as the formation of a Mizrachi workers' movement to work in agriculture and crafts in towns and villages. The latter proposal was entirely new and presaged the foundation of the Ha-Poel Ha-Mizrachi Movement. Even in those early days, Maimon realized the importance of a workers' movement within the Mizrachi organization.

Maimon's pragmatism was put to the test after his return to Palestine in 1919, shortly after the collapse of the Ottoman Empire. The League of Nations had given Britain Mandatory custody over Palestine, and one of the first matters to be dealt with was the jurisdiction of the rabbinical courts. A rabbinical council in Jerusalem that was intended to cover the whole country was established with Rabbi Kook as its leader. Maimon hoped that Rabbi Kook's messianic ideas would lead to the establishment of a Sanhedrin as the religious authority for the whole of world Jewry, and expressed this hope in speeches and in books throughout his life. It is surprising that as a politician dealing with the practical religious problems of the Yishuv and subsequently of the State of Israel, Maimon did not appreciate the futility of this proposal. Maimon also saw the establishment of rabbinical courts and a rabbinical council as steps along the road to the Yishuv's *political* independence and therefore as a development of fundamental importance. This shows clearly the integration of Judaism and political Zionism that was the hallmark of Maimon's thought and action throughout his life.

Maimon played a leading role in the heated debates regarding the incorporation of Jewish law in the Yishuv's communal life. His robust style enraged the secularist majority in the Zionist movement and sometimes made the Mizrachi itself uncomfortable, but his solid refusal to compromise on basic religious demands was at least partly responsible for achieving agreement that public agencies would observe Shabbat, festivals and kashrut. He realized that the Zionist leadership could not afford a break with Mizrachi.

At this time, Maimon tried to enlist the support of leading rabbis for the Mizrachi Movement, but met with little success. He viewed the Balfour Declaration as the first step to statehood, which was inevitable and must be fought for without compromise, and felt that Jewish law must be the law of such a state. Therefore, the struggle to lay a religious foundation for the state must be carried out from within the Zionist

Movement and the Va'ad Le'ummi, even though they each had a secular majority.

In addition, Maimon said that the basis of the religious Yishuv must be settlement and practical work in Palestine, together with the establishment of a network of religious schools. He embraced both the "practical" ideas of Ahad ha'Am, who stressed the development of a spiritual and material infrastructure for the country, as well as the approach of political Zionists whose energies were directed mainly at achieving political independence. These issues continued to dominate Maimon's political work from the time he became a member of the Jewish Agency Executive in 1935 to his term as Minister of Religions and War Victims in Israel's provisional government and first elected government, and continued until his withdrawal from political life.

Mizrachi's nomination of Maimon as its representative on the Executive of the Jewish Agency was received with unease by the existing members. A bitter opponent in religious matters over the years, he was considered to be uncompromising and difficult to work with. The nomination was accepted only out of deference to Mizrachi.

Maimon attended all meetings of the Agency Executive (which sat in Jerusalem) except when he was unwell or abroad, and over the years fought with the decisive support of Ben-Gurion for the implementation of the resolutions passed by the Zionist Movement for the communal observance of Shabbat, festivals and kashrut. By his persistence he was able, to a large extent, to avoid the real danger that these resolutions might in time become a dead letter as a result of persistent non-observance in practice.

In the course of time his integrity, devotion to Zionism and concern for all segments of the Jewish people, together with his considerable charm, when he chose to employ it, won him the respect of his colleagues (and Ben-Gurion's affection). His attachment to all sections of the Zionist Movement was made clear in a striking speech that he delivered to Mapai (the Labor Movement) in 1938. Mizrachi and Mapai maintained fundamental differences over the British government's proposal to partition Palestine – Mapai was prepared to accept the proposal while the

Mizrachi was vehemently opposed – and while Maimon did not minimize the differences that separated the groups, he pleaded that each party understand the views of the other. As for himself, he proclaimed: "If I had to choose between the unity of the people of Israel and the land of Israel, I would choose the people of Israel."

The minutes of the Jewish Agency Executive shed considerable light on Maimon's influence. Significantly, in the list of those present, his name usually appears next to that of the chairman, Ben-Gurion, and in the latter's absence he always acted as chairman. In effect, he was vice-chairman, though not in name, until the position was formalized, at which point he became joint vice-chairman.

Although Maimon's particular interest was in religious issues, he was also involved in social and economic matters which he considered to be equally the concern of Judaism (in an article in *Sinai,* he attacked the religious because they neglected the laws governing behavior between people). A few examples suffice to show this involvement. When the budget for aliyah was reduced, Maimon was quick to realize the potential increase in unemployment and demanded an increased budget for the Labor Department to maintain the level of employment. At the same time, he supported a proposal for a wage increase on the grounds that the cost of accommodation had risen, and the following year he was a member of the committee set up to deal with the problem of unemployment. Maimon was also concerned with the plight of the self-employed who were not covered by the Workers Sick Fund and participated in a committee to consider the allocation of funds to the unemployed. He subsequently headed a permanent committee to consider the interests of the middle class.

Relations with the Arabs and the Peel Report

The years 1936–1937 were traumatic for the Zionist Movement. In 1936, the British government suggested parity for Arab and Jew in the Mandatory government. Maimon opposed the proposal, maintaining the right of the Jews to the whole of Palestine. On the other hand, Ben-Gurion based his views on the decision of an earlier Zionist Congress that neither Jew nor Arab should control the other.

This issue came to a head upon the publication of the Peel Report in 1937. The British government proposed partitioning Palestine into two states, one Arab and one Jewish. Maimon opposed partition in principle, maintaining the Jewish right to the whole of Palestine. However, when it was clear that the government would not change its policy, Maimon agreed that the Agency should enter into negotiations so that the Jews would at least have one-half of the country. Surprisingly, Maimon suggested that in light of the situation, the Agency should consider dividing Jerusalem, with one part only inside the Jewish state.

It is interesting that Maimon had already realized the importance of considering Zionist policy towards the Arabs, suggesting the Agency should publish a newspaper in Arabic. However, he and Ben-Gurion agreed that the Jews would not be able to reach agreement with the Arabs and that the best solution was a Jewish state.

Against the background of the Peel Report, Arab riots throughout Palestine resulted in the deaths of hundreds of Jews. The Jewish Agency adopted a policy of restraint (in other words, non-retaliation) in response to the attacks, and Maimon said that the policy had failed – the number of immigration certificates had been reduced and none of the murderers had been caught.

Instead, he clashed strongly with Ben-Gurion, saying that one Arab should be killed for every Jewish victim, although he modified his views some months later. Regarding a group of young men from Rosh Pinnah who had been condemned to death for killing a British sergeant, Maimon said he would have condemned the judgment but nevertheless favored a policy of restraint. However, he said that the young men should not be in the same category as the Arab murderers whose acts had caused them to take vengeance.

Maimon made it clear that he condemned violence, and particularly Revisionist leader Ze'ev Jabotinsky, under whose inspiration the violent acts were committed. This was clearly illustrated in the 1948 *Altalena* incident, in which Haganah forces bombed an Irgun ship carrying arms and ammunition off the coast of Tel Aviv. The Irgun refused the Agency's demand to hand it over with its cargo, and Maimon (together with Shapira, head of the Mizrachi) suggested negotiations to reach a compromise, fearing a civil war that would critically endanger the fight for independence.

However, negotiations failed, and Maimon and Shapira resigned from the Agency when the *Altalena* was attacked. They returned shortly afterwards when, after blood had been spilled on both sides, the Irgun was defeated and the incident was over.

Maimon and Arab Rights

Maimon's views regarding partition and attitude toward the Arabs were surprisingly moderate in some respects. During the many discussions that were held on the rights of Arabs in a Jewish state, Maimon said that it was difficult for him to think in terms of restricting their right to buy land in view of the biblical injunction "There shall be a single law for the stranger and the citizen."

He insisted that Jews, who had experienced discrimination themselves, must not discriminate against another minority. However, there was one exception to the law of equal rights – a Jew was not allowed to sell land to a foreigner. With this exception, Arabs should have the same rights in a Jewish state as Diaspora Jews enjoyed in the countries where they lived – but there must be a Jewish state. He suggested that emigration of Arabs from the state might solve the problem, saying that it would be "a sin" to help Arabs settle in a Jewish state.

Agudat Israel

Nothing shows more clearly Maimon's devotion to Zionism than his approach to Agudat Israel, which over the years had opposed the Zionist Movement but nevertheless applied to join the Jewish Agency in 1939. Maimon objected to the application because the group had a history of opposing the Zionist Movement and also because Agudat Israel representatives wanted their own separate kosher slaughterhouses and schools, and demanded that the state be based on religious law.

Maimon was clear that no promises could be made on these matters, adding, "I am a political Zionist, and for me Zionism is one of the great things." Maimon wanted to hear Agudah's proposals about what form they felt the state should take before deciding on their application, but ironically he found himself a minority of one when the secular parties supported Agudah's inclusion.

Later, Maimon repeated that no undertaking should be given regarding religion because nothing had as yet been settled. His concern was clearly for the prospective state as a whole, and he seems to have felt that the Agudah would be a disruptive element in the life of the country by demanding special treatment beyond what had already been agreed between the religious and the secular parties.

The 1939 White Paper

Maimon called for an armed revolt against the British government policy limiting Jewish immigration to Palestine, which he felt was a breach of the government's obligation under the League of Nations mandate and the Balfour Declaration. Once the enormity of the Holocaust became clear, Maimon turned even more bitter over the government's refusal to allow unrestricted immigration. More than most, he realized the catastrophic loss not only of millions of Jews people but also of their leadership and their religious, cultural and communal traditions and identities.

The Biltmore Program

Maimon and Ben-Gurion became the outstanding protagonists for a Jewish state without compromise. At the Zionist Congress of America in 1942, held at the Biltmore Hotel in New York City, a program was to be adopted setting out Zionist aims. Maimon vigorously opposed the term *Kehillah Yehudit* for the proposed entity, arguing the phrase fell far short of a demand for a Jewish *state*. Together with Ben-Gurion, a compromise was reached to refer to the new country as a *medina* (a state) in Hebrew, but a commonwealth in English.

There can be little doubt that Maimon's objection to the original formula was tactically justified – one does not negotiate on the basis of a demand from which it is impossible to retreat without surrendering one's fundamental aims. In his case the original formula in effect went further

– it implicitly gave up the very demand for which Zionists had fought since the movement was established.

However, the issue strained relationships between the Agency Executive and Chaim Weizmann, the President of the World Zionist Organization, whom Maimon suspected of being too amenable to proposals that might prevent the establishment of a Jewish state. At one stage, after it appeared that Weizmann had been negotiating with the British government without consulting the Agency Executive, Ben-Gurion resigned and, at Maimon's suggestion he, Maimon, Moshe Sharet (then Shertok) and Dr. Shmorak went to London to meet Weizmann to insist on collective responsibility. The group met on February 14, 1944 in Dover, and Ben-Gurion resumed his chairmanship at the urging of his colleagues, most notably Maimon.

In the course of this visit to London, and subsequently to America in 1945, Maimon showed considerable diplomatic skills, smoothing the sometimes acerbic relations between Ben-Gurion and Weizmann and between the leading American Zionists Stephen S. Wise and Abba Hillel Silver, whose differences threatened the unity of the Zionist Organization of America. The fiery, uncompromising nominee of the Mizrachi to the Agency Executive had now become the conciliator.

The Revolt against British Administration

Maimon's militancy was not confined to the political arena. In his evidence at the trial of Irgun Zvai Leumi members accused of military training and possessing arms, Maimon said that the British government bore responsibility for the deaths of one million Jews and claimed the right to conduct military training in order to return Eretz Israel to the Jewish people.

Maimon almost always based his uncompromising demands on the principles of the Torah. In this way the religious basis for the claims of Zionism became an important consideration for the international community to take into account. Nor did he confine himself to speeches and writing. Maimon was a member of a Jewish Agency committee to consider and either approve or reject operations against the British recommended by the command of Tenuat Hameri (the Movement of the

Revolt). The committee approved the blowing up of all bridges between Palestine and adjoining countries in response to a proposal by a joint Anglo-American committee to create a bi-national state based on parity between Arabs and Jews under a United Nations Trusteeship.

In response, British authorities imprisoned leading members of the Agency, including Maimon. Upon his release he immediately joined Ben-Gurion, who was in Paris and needed his support on the issue of statehood against the moderates who had been strengthened by the Irgun's bombing attack of the King David Hotel that year. Maimon criticized the British government in the sharpest terms and demanded the dismissal of General Barker, who commanded the British troops in Palestine.

At the Twenty-Second Zionist Congress in 1946, Maimon supported Ben-Gurion's demand for the whole of Palestine as a Jewish state over Weizmann's objections. Maimon argued that although the Zionist movement had originally accepted the Peel Report's partition plan, once the Arabs had rejected it the Agency was free to revert to its original demand for the whole of the country. Maimon's speeches were praised by Stephen Wise, himself an outstanding orator, for their style and thorough intellectual integrity. He and Moshe Sneh were elected vice-chairmen of the World Zionist Organization's executive, and Ben-Gurion was elected chairman.

The End of the Mandate and Establishment of the State

On April 2, 1947, Britain passed the Palestine problem to the United Nations. Once again the Jewish Agency agreed to partition the land, but Maimon said that he would not appear before the United Nations unless he had permission to demand the whole of Palestine as a Jewish state. When the other members of the Agency Executive persisted in their disagreement, finally a compromise was reached in which Ben-Gurion would express the views of the majority and negotiate the details of partition, and Maimon would transmit the views of the religious demanding the whole country. Maimon, however, was a realist and when the United Nations voted for partition, he accepted the fact and even wrote welcoming the decision, noting the Jewish tradition that redemption would come step by step, and this was the beginning.

When the British withdrew on May 15, 1948 Maimon helped draft the Declaration of Independence, marking the occasion with a powerful speech in which he said, "From the days of Joshua until the last generation, for three thousand three hundred and eighteen years, Jewish settlement in Eretz Israel never ceased," adding that the hope of returning to Eretz Israel had never ceased either. Ben-Gurion read the Declaration aloud after which Maimon recited the *she-heheyanu* blessing: "Blessed are you, Lord our God, Sovereign of the Universe, who has kept us alive, sustained us and enabled us to reach this time."

Maimon wanted to establish Israel Independence Day as a full religious holiday with the same standing as the traditional festivals. This he did not achieve largely because of the indifference of the religious bodies involved in the decision. Nevertheless, the day became a secular holiday.

Following independence, Maimon's activities centered on the implementation of religious demands that had been the subject of decision by the Zionist Organization over the years, and also on the interests of the middle class. Even while he served as Minister of Religions, he continued to lead the Artisans and Retailers Department that had been set up during the Mandatory period. Maimon was tactful in his approach to colleagues and public institutions regarding breaches of Shabbat and *kashrut* regulations, and he had to point this out to religious detractors who felt that he was not forceful enough.

However, on some occasions, particularly regarding education, he recognized that he needed to employ the force of his fiery temperament. As Minister of Religion he played a decisive role in the dispute over the education of Yemenite children whose families had immigrated to Israel during Operation Magic Carpet in 1950. Maimon agreed to investigate the many complaints that these children were being given a secular education, in most cases against their parents' wishes. When the complaints were found to be justified, Maimon played a leading role in the subsequent bitter negotiations that resulted in an agreement with the ruling Labor Party ensuring that a religious education would be provided for the children of parents who wanted it.

As he had on other matters, Maimon clashed over this issue with Chief Rabbi Herzog, who demanded that all Yemenite children be given a religious education. This was a classic case of conflict between the religiously ideal solution over the practicalities of political life. Maimon knew the limitations of minority religious parties and realized the necessity of compromise if they were to remain in government, both in order to preserve what they had achieved religiously and to maintain the unity of its government in the early days of statehood.

Maimon also discussed the problem privately with Ben-Gurion, who was then prime minister, and it may be assumed that their rapport was a major factor in reaching an agreed solution.

One of Maimon's major achievements, together with Rabbi Shlomo Goren, the chief rabbi of the Israel Defense Force, was to prevent the formation of separate religious units or mess halls for religious soldiers in the army. Maimon felt that doing so would create a ghetto. Thanks to Ben-Gurion's support of Maimon and Goren, eventually the army brought together religious and non-religious soldiers, who otherwise had little contact with each other.

As soon as the first elected Knesset was formed on January 25, 1949, the government accepted the minimum religious demands of the religious parties that have formed the basis of the current status quo ever since. Maimon served in the government until 1952, when he resigned in order to devote himself to literary work.

Maimon and Ben-Gurion

The relationship between Ben-Gurion and Maimon was unusual and probably unique in Zionist history. The secularist and the rabbi not only worked harmoniously together, but also developed a true affection for each other. Their correspondence shows deep friendship, even when discussing matters on which they fundamentally differed. Warm greetings such as "My dear friend," "Your faithful friend," "My dear and honored friend," "With warm handshakes" and more are commonly found in letters between the two.

Six letters are of particular interest and illustrate their friendship and the strains to which it was inevitably exposed due to their fundamentally different views in relation to religion and state.

The first that illustrates most graphically the strength of their relationship was written by Ben-Gurion at the height of the Yemenite education crisis. After dealing with the issues on which they had serious differences, he wrote:

> I must tell you what is in my heart. I have been privileged to work with you in the foundation and building of the state and have learned to respect you as a worthy Jew, faithful Zionist and also as a fellow-worker and friend. It is not with an easy heart that I will part from you and your friends, and whatever happens in the political field your merit in my eyes will not change and my personal respect for you will not diminish. I know that you are a patriot no less than a party man, and for this reason I express my worries to you.

In a subsequent letter to Maimon, dated June 25, 1954, Ben-Gurion wrote that although he wanted Mizrachi and Ha-Poel ha-Mizrachi in the government, the majority in Israel were not religious and he stressed that there should be no coercion in the matter of religion either by the religious or the secular communities.

Ben-Gurion said that if all or the majority of the Jews were religious, he would accept a legal system for the state based on halacha, but this was not the case and the state must live by mutual tolerance. He pointed out that the Declaration of Independence specifically rejected the notion that halacha would be the law of the state. On the contrary, "We had declared that the state would not be a theocracy."

Four years later, Ben-Gurion wrote, "Many see themselves as part of the Jewish people even though they do not observe halacha. More than once it has been declared that this country is not based on halacha but on the law, but the law will not interfere on matters of halacha for those who are bound and live by it."

Maimon replied in kind, saying that although it had been agreed the state would not be a theocracy, it had also been agreed and declared that it would be a "'Jewish' state – a continuation of our historic nation connected to the tradition of its forebears." The term "Jewish," therefore, must be defined by Jewish tradition, as it had been during the Mandate.

In a long reply, Ben-Gurion repeated that the country was governed by the law, not by halacha, and defined the issue to be whether the laws of the state should be decided by the people or by religious law. In his view, it had been agreed in legislation, to which Maimon had subscribed, that it was permissible for the government to pass laws that were inconsistent with halacha.

Regarding the children of mixed marriages, Ben-Gurion maintained that parents had the right to decide whether or not they should be registered as Jews. At the end of the letter, Ben-Gurion expressed the hope that all who signed the Declaration of Independence would be faithful to the freedom of religion and conscience and avoid a *kulturkampf*. He wrote that while the state must provide for the needs of the religious, there must be no religious coercion.

The following year, Maimon referred to a letter sent by Ben-Gurion to a number of prominent thinkers, theologians and rabbis in which he asked them, "Who is a Jew?" Maimon felt the letter had made a terrible impression (as this question for millennia was decided only by Jewish law), particularly abroad, and he had been asked whether in these circumstances he would continue to celebrate Independence Day. He called on Ben-Gurion to correct the mistake that had caused such pain to hundreds of thousands of Jews.

This correspondence shows the dilemmas faced by a Jewish state based on democracy and the ideological irreconcilability between those who wanted a state based on halacha and those who maintained that while the religious should have freedom and facilities for their requirements, legislation should be only by the will of the majority.

One further letter (in 1954) should be quoted in particular to illustrate the purely personal aspect of their relationship. Ben-Gurion had moved to his new home in Sde Boker. After expressing regret that his health had prevented him from visiting him, Maimon continued:

By the way, in spite of the fact that in my opinion it was not necessary for you to leave Jerusalem, when I read your words in the press that you had become a partner with God in your work, I thought the step you had taken was appropriate – but only if you will be His partner.

In practice, Ben-Gurion and Maimon had pointed to the only way in which, despite these differences, the secular and religious could live together. Their discussions were free of invective and personal attacks, and over the years they gradually reached a *modus vivendi* as neither was overly influenced by extremists on each side of the ideological spectrum. Subsequently, the leaders of Mizrachi and Ha-Poel ha-Mizrachi became members of successive Labor governments during the early formative years of statehood.

What were the elements that created a close relationship between Ben-Gurion and Maimon? Perhaps, above all, Ben-Gurion saw in Maimon a unique phenomenon in Jewish public life – the Jew rooted in the traditions of the Eastern European shtetl who not only had a love for the Land of Israel but was free of the *galut* (exile) mentality that so often prevented Jewish leaders from confronting governments when necessary to preserve or achieve Jewish rights.

Moreover, Ben-Gurion found in Maimon a staunch ally in the fight for a Jewish state without compromise. He also appreciated Maimon's concern for all sections of the Yishuv, religious and secular. In turn, Maimon valued Ben-Gurion's support for the incorporation of basic halachic requirements in the laws of the Jewish state.

Finally, the two men had common scholarly interests. Each of them had a very large library, and Ben-Gurion particularly appreciated the forty thousand volumes of Maimon's collection, which included outstanding and rare manuscripts and early printed works.

It is almost impossible to imagine such a friendship at the close of the first decade of the twenty-first century. Perhaps the best example of this friendship may be seen in a personal letter that Ben-Gurion wrote to Maimon after the latter resigned from the Knesset. "My dear friend… what I said on that occasion is only a part of the respect and love I have for you, because no man can reveal his heart in public. You were dear to me the whole time I was privileged to work with you and were seven times as dear to me during the period of statehood."

The personality that emerges from this brief account of Maimon's political life is of a religious Zionist whose allegiance to the Zionist Movement and its aims was complete and unswerving, a fighter for the establishment of a Jewish state with religious content, the devoted and active vice-chairman of the Jewish Agency Executive. He was quick to lambast, sometimes rather sharply, those policies with which he disagreed, but was nevertheless willing to compromise if it was impossible to achieve his aims in full, particularly if it was necessary in order to maintain the unity of the Jewish people. He also had a charisma that he used effectively from time to time, as we have seen. Above all, he was a man of integrity who loved the entire Jewish people.

Did Maimon have a decisive voice in Zionism? The Agency minutes do not indicate any contribution by him to financial or economic discussion. Although, as we have shown, he expressed concern when policies threatened the working class and he became the chairman of a committee whose task was to protect the interests of the self-employed, his overall influence, judging by his files in the Zionist archives, was not considerable. Even in specifically religious matters it is easy to exaggerate his influence. By the time he joined the Agency Executive there had already been broad agreement to Mizrachi's basic religious demands.

Nevertheless, Maimon's strong insistence on the implementation of the Zionist Organization's resolutions on religious matters ensured that they would constitute the religious foundation of the Yishuv and, later, the state. However, there were two aspects in which Maimon made a valuable and unique contribution to Zionism: with the possible exception of Ben-Gurion, he was the most consistent robust and eloquent advocate of Jewish statehood in the Zionist Movement. More than anyone else, he was the embodiment of religious Zionism: rooted in tradition but sensitive to the needs and interests of a modern and largely secular society.

It is appropriate to sum up Maimon's influence on Zionism and the State of Israel with the words of Ben-Gurion on the occasion of his resignation from the Knesset.

> I wish to say a few words about my colleague and dear teacher Rabbi Maimon. I have had the privilege of working with him for more than sixteen years, though I have known him for over forty years. It has not been easy to work with him, for Rabbi Maimon is a tough, stubborn, zealous man who defends his views vigorously and militantly, and in this respect has not changed to this day. It is amidst strife and conflict that we have learned to appreciate him. I know no other man among the veteran members of the Movement who arouses greater feelings of respect and trust in his exalted faith and moral views, which would do honor to any good socialist.

> I have had the privilege of working with him not only for many years in the Zionist Executive but also in the Government of Israel ever since the formation of the provisional government, and perhaps no one in the government has caused me more headaches. But never have I accepted more troubles with more love than those that he caused, for I love this man with all my heart for his profound Zionist faith and his pure and perfect love of Israel, his unbounded loyalty to the state, and his great concern for the well being of the nation and the state.

ABOUT THE AUTHOR

RAYMOND GOLDWATER has been active in Anglo-Jewish affairs for many years. After graduating in law at the University of London, he was Chairman of the Inter-University Jewish Federation of Great Britain in 1939–1940. For nineteen years he was an honorary officer of the United Synagogue of London, the largest synagogue body in Great Britain comprising more than thirty thousand members, and served as chairman of both its welfare and publication committees. A former chairman of the University Chaplaincy Board for Jewish students and of the Religious Advisory Committee of the Association for Jewish Youth, he contributed articles to *Le'ela,* a periodical published by the London School of Jewish Studies, and served as editor of *Jewish Philosophy and Philosophers,* published by the Hillel Foundation of Great Britain.